SPEAKING
without fear

Dale L.
Minnick CSP*

*Certified Speaking Professional

Speaking Without Fear

Dale L. Minnick, CSP*
* Certified Speaking Professional

Copyright © MCMXCV

Printed in the United States of America

Typesetting by Ad Graphics of Tulsa

Library of Congress Catalog Card Number: 95-70307

ISBN 0-9633476-8-3

For information contact:
Dale Minnick
P. O. Box 785
Woodward, OK 73802

Speaking Without Fear

Dedication

This book is dedicated to my father and mother, Leslie and Coralee Minnick, who celebrated 53 years of marriage as this book is finished.

I also want to acknowledge the many great speakers who had a positive influence on my life. Thanks, also, to the tens of thousands of people who have been in my audiences. Thanks for your laughter, your tears, your applause, your compliments, and your encouragement.

Finally, I wish to acknowledge the guidance and love of my beautiful wife, Laura, and the patience and support of our four great children, Greg, Sarah, Sage, and Dallyn. Thanks to Cheryl for all the long hours on the word processor. And thanks to my God for this gift of speaking and the opportunities to use that gift.

Introduction And Acknowledgment

This book has been written especially for you, with the help of many, many people. It's designed to help you learn from my mistakes and experiences, without all the pain. I wish I'd had this book 20 years ago.

Between the covers of this book are hundreds of practical, "How To" ideas for you to put to instant use. The material has been gleaned from my personal experiences, mistakes, and personal observations of almost 20 years of public speaking.

The humor collection contained in this book is one I began assembling in 1975. The entries come from a variety of sources, many long forgotten and some never known. They've been clipped, cut out, torn, ripped, and rewritten on odd pieces of paper and that's the way they came out of my file. In addition, there are many personal humor stories I know will fit your life. My thanks to the many friends, speakers, and authors who contributed to this collection.

There are several unique approaches in this book you won't find anywhere else. The Audience Potential Index is my brainchild to help you and me do a better job controlling the outcome of our presentations.

Another unique aspect is the organization of "How To" and humor materials into various periods of your life. Developing personal stories, building personal humor lines, and using humor from the collections at the back will each be easier and more effective using this method than any other method I know about.

There's something in this book for everyone...even those who find great delight in discovering spelling errors and punctuation mistakes. In fact, if you spot one we didn't put in on purpose, write and tell us.

Finally, this book does not contain all the answers. No one volume can contain everything you need to know and do. But it does contain the items I believe have the greatest impact on your ability to speak without fear!

CHAPTER I

HELP!!! I'VE GOT TO GIVE A SPEECH

– Face your fears and succeed.

I'M SC-SC-SCARED!

Speaking in public still ranks as the number one fear of most people on the face of the planet.

The most frequent comment I hear is "I don't see how you can get up there and do that — if I had to I'd just die!" Believe it or not, history only records one death from public speaking. President William Henry Harrison caught pneumonia giving a 2-hour inaugural speech in the rain and died after his first 31 days in office.

Let me put your fears at rest. All professional speakers started just like you did — with unintelligible sounds, a few goo-goo-ga-gas and then the first word. Somewhere beyond that, about the first grade, we watched some poor classmate freeze up in front of the whole world at the Christmas program and we decided that speaking in public and self-humiliation were one-and-the-same.

Everyone I know gets a few butterflies in their stomach before they speak. As a fellow speaker puts it, the only difference between an amateur and a professional is that the professional knows how to get his butterflies to fly in formation! So let's put some of your butterflies in formation.

YOU'RE ALREADY A PUBLIC SPEAKER

Unless you are a total recluse, you already speak in public. When you talk to business associates, make sales calls, order at a restaurant, or even yell at the kids to come home for dinner, you're a "public" speaker.

And just like all public speakers, people listen to what you say, notice how you look, look at how you gesture, listen to how you say your words, see how comfortable you are, and take note of how funny you are.

There are many more people listening to you every day than you ever imagined. In other words, you already have audiences, whether you want to admit it or not.

In fact, you already give several "hot topic" speeches every day. You speak about Time Management when you exchange daily plans with your spouse. You speak about Motivation when you tell your kids why they need to be home on time. You speak on Accomplishment when you plan with employees about how that new project should unfold. You also speak about Selling, Inspiration, and probably even Humor (ever share a funny story or a joke with someone?).

YOUR FEARS ARE NORMAL

Actually, most of us are already fairly polished public speakers with some pretty good material, but we get extremely frightened at the thought of doing that material up in front of a crowd. Why is that? Simple. It's because we're scared we'll lay an egg, be a bomb, oversweat, under-think, forget our words, trip on our tongue, and probably humiliate ourselves forever! And with all those negative goals on our minds, we usually make a few of them come true.

Those fears are normal. In fact, many polished professional speakers who make a living speaking have some of the same fears before most presentations. No matter how many speeches they've given, compliments they've heard, or standing ovations they've received, almost every speaker fears that the next one might be the "killer".

I'll talk about some of the "killers" I've had later in this book, but let me assure you of one thing, they will happen. And just as they occasionally occur in front of a crowd, they also occur in day-to-day conversations.

We've all flopped at one time or another in making a statement in public, embarrassed ourselves, and contemplated a tonguectomy. We've all heard comments like "I know you must have some great thoughts and ideas...it's too bad they never make it to your mouth!"

But, think with me a second. Why is it that most people keep on trying to learn to walk, ride a bike, or ski, but quietly give up on public speaking? Usually it's because of external peer and family pressure. We hear "Keep trying son, you'll make it", when we're learning to walk. Or we hear "Gee, Tom, if you'd learn to ski better we could ski with those two blondes". All positive input. Everybody wants to see us walk, bike, and ski.

But what do we hear when we mess up in front of a crowd? All negative, "You blew that!". Or worse...dead silence and blank stares. Or even worse, people get up and leave! No wonder we hate to get up in front of a crowd!

EVERY GREAT SPEAKER STARTED AT THE BOTTOM

Every successful well-known speaker I know started out as

an amateur. As a beginner, they gave a first speech, a second speech, and a third. And every one of them at one point in their life was right where you are today.

THE GREATEST SKILL YOU CAN POSSESS

Developing highly effective speaking skills can move people farther and faster up the ladder of success than almost any other talent they possess. There is no question that excellent speakers are given credit for being far more intelligent than "non-speakers". Plus, their developed ability to "think on their feet" makes them top choices for leadership positions in all walks of life.

YOU COULD BE DRAFTED INTO THE PROS

Strangely enough, most speakers I have met who are now very successful in their professional speaking careers came from some other background. They came to speaking from a variety of fields including farming, furniture stores, university faculties, beauty salons...backgrounds just like yours. Many of these people also failed in their former professions. Others developed successful speaking careers concurrently with their profession. Some professional speakers continue to carry on another profession in addition to their speaking business. Every speaker I ever met came to professional speaking from some other avenue or from some other profession...and that's what makes them unique. Just like you.

In many cases the road to professional speaking starts with a simple request by a superior, or a co-worker, or a neighbor, or a fellow church worker to make a presentation. One of the most successful speakers in the industry had a furniture store in dire financial straits due to a closing military installation. He was asked to prepare a leadership seminar for his church. That request by his pastor led him to many that followed and eventually to his developing a sales education program adopted by one of the largest corporations in America. He started just where you are today.

THIS BOOK WILL HELP YOU

So, whether you are about to make your very first presentation to a public audience, or you are somewhere past that point and have been considering becoming a full-time professional speaker, this book is for you. Each chapter has been designed to help you get your butterflies into formation, starting from right where you are today. As a friend of mine is fond of saying, "You don't have to be good to start, but you do have to start to be good." So let's get started learning more about how to speak without fear.

CHAPTER II

MAKE ME LAUGH

– Never use humor–unless you want the audience to like you.

HUMOR

I believe every good speech I've ever heard was good because it contained humor. Most "bad" speeches I've heard could have been better if they had included humor.

Humor is a powerful medicine, a pain killer, a life extender, a healing tool for the sick, and a stimulant for the depressed. Studies show that only 15 seconds of laughter adds 2 days to your life span.

Humor can also come from your own personal experiences, from others' personal experiences, or from a humor source such as this book. I'll show you how to develop your own personal humor in a minute, but before I do, let me briefly explain how to use the humor section in the back of this book.

464 humor entries have been included, beginning in Chapter 16. These humorous entries have been organized to correspond with the 24 periods of your life. For example, if you're in a hurry and need a story about marriage to complement your own experience, turn to the Humor Index on page 104. Find the category "Marriage", turn to that

page, and there you will find several humor entries on the subject of marriage from which to choose.

Plus, I've added four more categories just because there's so much good material about them. They are Farmers & Ranchers; Lawyers; Old Age; and Politicians.

DEVELOPING YOUR OWN HUMOR

Let me share with you an easy way to develop your own humor. In fact, with this simple method you can take one of your own personal experiences and expand it into a 10-minute routine, or perhaps an entire presentation.

First, select a topic. Maybe that topic is "My Most Painful Experience". Maybe it was an experience that really hurt (remember that tragedy + time = humor). Maybe it will be a news object like the President of the United States, a sports scandal, or some other significant event that most of your audience will easily recognize and identify with.

Now once you've selected a topic, I want you to look at it from several different "angles". To help you, I've listed below six different "angles" to look at your topic. Look at your topic from each "angle" and write down the most specific details you can recall about each.

For example, I'll pick Texas as my topic and I'll write down some examples under each "angle".

1. The People Involved
(Your details will include things like names, ages, clothing, relatives, pets, houses, character, integrity, known problems, hair, baldness, features, and so on.)
Here's my list: **Sam Houston, Governor Ann Richards, Texas Rangers, Dallas Cowboys, Houston Oilers, John Connally, John F. Kennedy, Lyndon Johnson, Lady Bird Johnson, George Bush, Millionaires, oil men, Hunt Brothers.**

2. The Places

(Where the incident took place, others like it, location, time of year, background, history, weather, and so on.) *Dallas, The Alamo, Texas A&M, Austin, University of Texas, ranches, oil fields, Fort Worth, Mexican border.*

3. The Things

(What objects were present; cars, guns, desks, bottles, skates, bats, ink pens, car radios, and so on.) *Football, oil, cattle, ranches, immigration, drought, piney woods, bank failures, elections, flag, DFW airport.*

4. The Events

(What events led to this event, how did this event unfold step by step.) *War with Mexico, oil boom, oil bust, football games, assassinations, banking scandals, Aggie Yell practice.*

5. The Words

(What was said, by whom, dialects involved, phrases used, cute sayings, mis-used words, off-scene conversations, voices, pitch, screams, shouts, crying, and so on.) *Lone Star State, Remember the Alamo, Horns, Who Shot J.R., Republic of Texas.*

6. The Action

(How people gestured, walked, sat down, used their hands, touched themselves, touched others, ran, jumped, fell, and so on.) *Beggars on street, proud Texans, fancy parties, state government scandals, Loss at the Alamo, growing Hispanic population, throwing money around, Kennedy's assassination, University of Texas playing University of Oklahoma.*

Now let's look at some of the lines I came up with immediately after using this method.

> *My introducer is a devout Texas A&M fan, he has a bumper sticker on his car that says, "Honk if I'm an Aggie"...And the bumper sticker's on top of his car.*

I was really impressed with your emcee tonight when he told me about his family's great Texas heritage, that one of his ancestors was killed in the Alamo. Then I talked to his wife and found out it was the Alamo Motel in Amarillo.

The Dallas Cowboys are America's team. They're coming out of one of their worst seasons ever, which should give you an idea of what terrible shape America's been in.

A friend of mine back home is a retired Texas Banker. A Texas judge retired him.

I was in a small town in a East Texas cafe last week when a stranger walked in and yelled, "The President is a horse's rear." Three good old boys stalked towards him when he yelled "This is a free country. I can say what I want about the President." One of the good old boys said, "You don't understand, this is horse country."

It's always great to read about your state legislature. There's some really smart people in Austin and some really dumb people. Only problem is you can't tell 'em apart.

I didn't know how bad the oil business had gotten. In downtown Houston last week I saw a guy in a three-piece suit standing on the corner holding a sign that said, "Will trade oil leases for diapers."

Now study each item and play "what if" games. What if some out-of-the place person would have been there (like Elvis). What if the place had been different or it had been raining. Let your imagination run wild and don't be afraid to embellish each item to add to its humorous effect.

One of the quickest and most fun ways to develop humor for your speech is to combine a true personal experience from your list with a humor entry from this book or another source. That is, take you real life situation and fit the humor entry to that experience. Be careful, though. After you tell the story a few times, you'll start believing it really happened.

I prefer to take a serious situation or message, make my point, then reinforce it with humor. Here's an example:

1. Make your point. *"We all need to look at the opportunities that exist right in our own back yard."*

2. Incorporate a personal experience. *"I grew up in a small town, but one full of people who were always looking for opportunities."*

3. Reinforce with humor. *"In fact, we're building a new Senior Citizen's center back home....with a maternity wing."*

4. Restate the point. *"Look for opportunities."*

Humor should always be clean. I have never heard any meeting planner compliment a speaker for his or her ability to use off-color humor. I have often heard complaints from meeting planners about speakers who did use off-color humor. And I have booked many engagements because the other contender had a reputation for being too racy. My personal policy is never to use a story I would not want my children to hear. The greatest compliment I can receive is "I don't understand how you can be so funny and so clean!"

TYPES OF HUMOR

Humor material can be divided into several types.

1. Situational Humor
2. Topical Humor
3. Unexpected punch line
4. Satire
5. Exaggeration or embellishment
6. One-liners like Bob Hope uses
7. Ad Libs or Asides
8. Inconsistent Comparisons
9. Jokes
10. Personal Experiences
11. Poetry
12. Puns
13. Stories
14. Insult Humor

Almost everyone has a favorite humor story that "always" gets a laugh. Build up to it with two or three stories with small laughs so that you build into your big laugh punch line...1st small laugh, 2nd small laugh, 3rd small laugh, then the big laugh.

Ad-libs or "asides" are also extremely effective to slip into a story. While some speakers can pull them off impromptu, I prefer planning my "asides". I put them in on purpose, but make them look like they were unplanned.

For example, I tell a story about one of my children being in a wedding. I start off, "We had a big fancy wedding back home the other day and they asked my 5-year-old son to be in it." To beef up my line I might add a planned ad lib line as follows, "We had a big fancy wedding back home the other day...(pause)...it was one of these nice ones...where everybody agreed to it...(pause)...(wait for laughter to start subsiding)...They asked my 5-year-old son to be in it....

Another old ad-lib widely used but still very effective is when someone coughs or sneezes very noticeably. Stop where you are and say "My uncle died from a cough like that...'course he was in another man's closet at the time".

Finally, let me briefly convince you of the effectiveness of situational humor — the delivery of a line that will probably only fit that one situation. I owe my initial success as a speaker to one opening line at a convention in Albuqurque in 1979 that literally brought down the house and took over 2 minutes to get the audience of 600 to settle down. I thought of the line on the way to the stage. And if I were to describe it here it probably wouldn't even sound funny — it was appropriate for only that one time and one situation. If you can find that one humorous story or line that ties together that one something that's on everyone's mind, and deliver it well, you will be UP IN FRONT a lot!

TIMING

Wait for the laughter. I've heard lots of great humorous presentations where the speaker was just a little too "wired". When he didn't get an immediate response to his story, he went right into the next one.

The unfortunate result is that people were just ready to laugh, but when the speaker went on they suppressed the laughter in order to not miss the next story. Give the audience time to respond. Some people don't "catch" things quickly, and some audiences are slower than others. Deliver your punchline, fix your expressions, and wait.

Also, don't be disappointed if an audience doesn't giggle uncontrollably at all of your stories. I know from personal experience you can give the same speech to similar audiences in the same part of the country and some stories will be great one night and not the next (and vice versa).

Noted humorist Doc Blakely gave me some great advice in this area. He said "If they don't laugh, don't act like they were supposed to." Continue on.

The flip side of this is that you will also probably get laughs you hadn't planned on. Never act like you weren't expecting them. In fact, when you get a laugh you weren't expecting, study the tone of your voice, the timing, and the words you used. You have just found a new "ad-lib" that you can put in on purpose next time to add to the laughs.

To paraphrase an old question, "How do you get UP IN FRONT to the microphone?" Practice, practice, practice. Rehearse your lines. Try them every chance you get. Act like you just got your life insurance license — try to sell everyone you know. I'm still refining and building on to stories I used 10 years ago. Keep practicing.

CHAPTER III

THE AUDIENCE POTENTIAL INDEX

– 75% of the success of your speech has nothing to do with what you say.

NO CONTROL

I believe one of the primary reasons people shy away from speaking in public is that they feel so "without control". They think "I've got to get up there in front of those people and I have no control over whether they like me or accept what I say."

If I could show you a way you could take control of your audience and squeeze every drop of potential out of them, would you want to know about it? Please say yes! Good, but before I do, let me relate to you my "dollar-size" example about taking control.

Years ago I spent several years as an officer of a large financial institution. Each Tuesday morning we had a management meeting where the senior officers would go around the table and discuss the previous week's activities, plus upcoming events, and present other reports.

During one period of weeks, we began to notice our savings

deposits were consistently sliding. We had several large withdrawals. When asked "why", the Vice President of Savings responded by telling us that we were experiencing problems with our new computer system. Customers were coming in, asking for the balance in their savings accounts, and our tellers couldn't tell them...because our computer was "down".

Naturally, our customers were saying things like, "I've got over $100,000 in here of my life's savings, and you can't even tell me exactly how much I have?" And our tellers were saying, "No, I can't, the computer's down." The customer went away mad and in many cases took his money with him...down the street...to our competition.

"So, you see," said the Vice President, "it's the computers fault we're losing all this money." What she was saying is "We don't have any control over this situation."

Prior to the next management meeting I determined our computer problems were going to continue for at least another month and suggested a temporary policy change which was implemented. Here's the policy:

> When someone comes in and we can't tell them how much money they have in their account due to computer difficulty, we do the following:
>
> 1) Explain that our computer is temporarily down
>
> 2) Find out where they could be reached personally or by phone in the next hour
>
> 3) Offer to call, hand carry, or mail the appropriate information
>
> 4) Slide a $10 bill across the counter and explain "It's our policy when this happens that we award you $10 for having to wait for your information."

What happened? Customers started coming in "wanting" the computer to be down. Some would even slide the money back and say that wasn't necessary. We didn't spend more than $1,000 on the solution and it saved us millions in account withdrawals. We succeeded by taking control. Now let me show you how to succeed and speak without fear by taking control.

TAKE CONTROL OF YOUR SPEAKING EVENT

I hear speakers say time and time again, "I'd a done better, but...it wasn't a good crowd, the sound system wasn't turned up, the emcee messed up my introduction," and on and on why their presentation was not successful.

You as a speaker owe it to your meeting planner, your audience, and yourself to take control of every item in your power that will make yours a successful presentation.

The "potential" of every audience you speak to is in your hands, not theirs. Take control of realizing that potential. To help you, I've developed the AUDIENCE POTENTIAL INDEX or API for speakers. Putting the API to work will result in greater appreciation, more return engagements, and greater long-term success for you as a speaker.

THE AUDIENCE POTENTIAL INDEX
(API) FOR SPEAKERS

The Audience Potential Index is designed to help you learn about the items you can control and to allow you to check them off before and after your presentation to see if you did everything in your power to make your speech successful.

The Audience Potential Index consists of 10 steps, in the order they would normally occur in a speaking event. Please note that none of these items relate to your material or its delivery. You already have control over your speech (if not, everything you say may be a big surprise, too!).

THE AUDIENCE POTENTIAL INDEX SCORE SHEET

	API Score Points	YOUR Score Points

STEP 1. TAKE CONTROL AFTER THE BOOKING AND BEFORE THE ENGAGEMENT DATE

Mail Questionaire for meeting planner and get it back completed .... 60 _____

Mail Thank you card for return of questionaire ...... 25 _____

Thank you call for questionaire and responses .... 25 _____

BONUS: Personal visit with meeting planner before meeting .... 60 _____

BONUS: On-site educational visit .... 50 _____

BONUS: Find out who the Board members, officers and head table guests are and write them a letter beforehand telling them how much you're looking forward to being with them .... 40 _____

Call one week before to confirm your travel plans and ask about any recent changes in the organization or people .... 50 _____

Call meeting planner upon arrival at hotel or meeting location to notify them that you are there .... 50 _____

STEP 2. TAKE CONTROL WHEN YOU ARRIVE

Arrive at meeting early .... 25 _____

Find the meeting planner .... 25 _____

BONUS: Sit in on other parts of the program .... 40 _____

Locate the meeting room in advance .... 25 _____

STEP 3. TAKE CONTROL CHECK OUT THE SOUND SYSTEM

Find out who is in charge of the sound system .... 30 _____

Check the sound system for volume and tone .... 30 _____

Check the sound system for dead spots .... 30 _____

Check the microphone location and how to turn it on 20 _____

Check the microphone cord for length, where it is plugged in, shake it and turn it on to make sure you can move around and it doesn't come apart .... 20 _____

Ask for reasonable changes in the sound system.... 50 _____

Before you're introduced, walk around the room & listen to the sound .... 40 _____

Take your own microphone with you .... 30 _____

STEP 4. TAKE CONTROL OF THE LIGHTING

Find out who is in charge of the lighting system ..... 20 _____

Check for the location of controls, and test them.... 20 _____

Look for burned out lights and resulting dark spots in the room .... 20 _____

Make sure flood and spot lights are pointed where you want them .... 20 _____

STEP 5. TAKE CONTROL OF THE MEETING ROOM

Find out who's next door and when they'll be doing what .... 60 _____

Ask for sections to be roped off to force people to the front where you want them .... 30 _____

Stand at the lectern and check for proper height and check location of note holders .... 40 _____

Find out who is in charge of seating arrangement .. 35 _____

Determine if tables are too far away or too close ..... 50 _____

Ask that tables be moved if necessary and offer to help 70 _____

Find out who will be at the head table .... 35 _____

STEP 6. TAKE CONTROL OF YOUR INTRODUCTION

Find out who will be introducing you .... 50 _____

Introduce yourself to the introducer .... 60 _____

Make sure he/she has a copy of your introduction . 60 _____

Find out as much as you can about your introducer 30 _____

Specify that they read the introduction as you have written .... 30 _____

Carry an extra copy of your introduction to provide if necessary .... 40 _____

STEP 7. GREET YOUR AUDIENCE —
TAKE CONTROL
Find out where people will be arriving and place yourself at the door to greet as many as possible ... 50 _____

If there is a buffet line, get at the head of the line, hand out plates and introduce yourself .... 60 _____

Place yourself by the registration desk and introduce yourself to them as they register .... 50 _____

Walk around and introduce yourself to each member at the head table and ask them about themselves .. 60 _____

Once they're seated, go out in the audience, shake hands, greet them, ask where they're from, what they do, joke with them, thank them for coming .... 70 _____

STEP 8. AFTER YOU ARE INTRODUCED —
TAKE CONTROL
BONUS: After you're introduced, if people are at the back, ask them to move in a creative way .... 60 _____

For seminars, take an extra copy of your overheads, and an extra bulb for the projector .... 20 _____

Go to where the people are, if they won't come to you, you've got to go to them .... 50 _____

Always thank the meeting planner, the board, and the introducer before you reach the end of your presentation and encourage the audience to thank them too .... 50 _____

BONUS: Ask for a round of applause for the meeting planner for all their efforts for a great meeting .... 50 _____

STEP 9. AFTER YOUR SPEECH —
TAKE CONTROL
After you conclude stay at the microphone and say Thank You three times with pauses in between ...... 40 _____

Wave or bow to to the audience before or just after you leave the lectern .... 30 _____

As you move toward your seat, shake hands with your introducer .... 35 _____

Place yourself at the exit or otherwise make yourself available to as many people as possible afterward .. 40 _____

Linger until the last possible minute to visit and exchange cards or brochures .... 30 _____

Personally thank the Board members, the President and the meeting planner again for inviting you ...... 50 _____

STEP 10. TAKE CONTROL OF THE FOLLOW-UP

Upon returning home, write "nice to meet you" letters to people you met .... 50 _____

Write Thank You letters to the Board and officers and commend the great job done by the meeting planner and any others in authority. Mention them personnally in the letter .... 60 _____

Send the meeting planner a gift (cup, flowers, etc.). 50 _____

TOTAL POINTS **2,000**

TOTAL WITH BONUS POINTS **2,300**

SCORING YOUR PRESENTATIONS

If you consistently score 1600 to 2000 points or more on your speaking engagements, you're doing a great job of squeezing all the potential out of your audiences. Give yourself an A.

If you consistently score 1200 to 1600 points you've got most of it mastered, but you're probably not getting everything you could out of your audiences. Give yourself a B.

A score between 800 to 1200 indicates you're missing out on repeat perfomances, and giving up lots of future income by not giving all you can. Give yourself a C.

A score below 800 is a danger sign. You need to work on your self-confidence in working with meeting planners and audience members alike. It also indicates your long-term speaking career may be in jeopardy without some serious bold moves. (Or it could mean you're a celebrity speaker. If so, what are you doing with a copy of my book, write your own!)

CHAPTER IV

YOUR ROOM OR MINE

– The closer they are, the better you look.

THE "KILLER" SPEECH

San Angelo, Texas, several years ago. Almost 250 in a room that would have held 1,000. Enough tables for 600. People scattered everywhere, eating catfish from a buffet line.

Head table is twenty feet above the main floor (seemed like it) ornately decorated with a five feet wide lectern. Almost 30 of the 250 people were at the head table. Nearest person in the audience was 50 feet away...with a video camera!

The meeting planner's words just before the meeting still ring in my ears, "Last guy we had for a speaker was from Louisiana, Cajun fella, and he didn't go over too good. That was 10 years ago and we ain't had another speaker till you."

I was so far away and so far up above that thin, scattered group, I almost asked them to stand up and stay standing...cause everything I was saying was going right over their heads!!

That was almost my last speech—I don't know if that "Cajun fella" is still around but I almost quit for good that sleepless night back in the motel. In fact, after returning home from that speech I mailed the check back with a letter advising them to hire a band for the next 20 years! I've often thought the National Speakers Association should have sent that guy an award for not hiring more than 2 speakers in 11 years.

Before I leave my "bomb" story I should tell you that every problem could have been corrected. Getting a long mike cord, moving down off the stage, asking the people to move to the front, and taking the trouble to work the crowd beforehand would have solved most of my problems.

Why didn't I recognize the potential problems? I did recognize them. I simply thought I was good enough to overcome them. I was wrong. I wish I had known then about an Audience Potential Index and about taking control of the meeting room. Let's talk a little more about Step 5 of the Audience Potential Index, Taking Control of the Meeting Room.

MY IDEAL ROOM SET-UP

If I were able to list meeting room arrangements for a banquet speech in order of my preference it would be as follows:

1) Banquet-style, long tables

2) Theater style

3) Classroom style

4) Banquet-style, round tables

Regardless of the arrangement, the tighter they're grouped, the better their response, even in a large room not fully utilized. Low ceilings are better than high ceilings because the sound goes up. Responses are contagious and if they can hear laughter around them, they'll laugh longer and more often.

If I could pick the "ideal" room arrangement to achieve the highest Audience Potential Index possible it would be as follows:

1) Banquet style with long tables running perpendicular to a head table.

2) People seated on both sides of the banquet table.

3) The room is packed.

4) A riser in front of the lectern equal in height to the platform at the head table. (Riser usually not needed in groups of less than 150-200.)

5) A long microphone cord or wireless hand-held mike.

This style is most conducive to "packin' 'em" in. The reason for the riser in number 4 is that I typically speak from in front of the head table. I want to be close to the audience because I use people from the audience in the presentation. In large audiences and in unusually wide or unusually long rooms, the riser will put you up where you may be seen by those stuck off in the corners and back rows.

THE WORST ROOM SET-UP

If I could pick the worst arrangement which would render the least audience response and the lowest API, it would be as follows:

1) Round tables 10-15 feet apart.

2) Room is half full of tables, and the tables only half full of people, some are empty.

3) No head tables, no lectern, nothing to indicate a "head" of the room.

4) Or worse yet, a head table present, but it's four feet off the main floor and the nearest person in your audience is 50 feet away.

5) A microphone fixed to a lectern with one or two feet of cord.

Most speakers will tell you they are at the mercy of the meeting planner when it comes to the room arrangement. That's not true. Specify your desired room arrangement in your letter of agreement when you book the speech and simply drop this line "the closer they're seated together, the more responsive they'll be." You may even want to make that suggestion again when you check the room before your speech. And always, always check the room before you speak. Many times it won't be set up before you check it and you can get it exactly the way you want it. But always check it out, and don't rely on the meeting planner. I've had meeting planners fail to check the room themselves and walk in to find an arrangement that took them by surprise.

Meeting planners are extremely busy. At their meetings they are not only besieged with hundreds of little logistical problems, they're dealing with the politics and personalities of their boards, executives, members, etc. I've found meeting planners almost always receptive to any ideas that will make your presentation go better. Plus, if you volunteer to help and make sure it gets done, they're even more receptive.

GET THEM ELBOW TO ELBOW

A popular country-western song contains the line "The closer you get, the further I fall". I'm sure the lyricist refers to falling in love or meeting someone who hasn't bathed for a while. But when it comes to audiences, the line might more appropriately read "The closer you get, the more responsive you'll be".

A "packed house" or a crowded seating arrangement will always be the most receptive, responsive audience. Why? I believe it's because in "packed houses" each person's comfort zone is violated. They are uncomfortable, if only slightly.

My experience indicates people will laugh more, cry easier, and give more standing ovations, if they're seated in close quarters. Interestingly, laughing and sharing that experience with a stranger who's violating their comfort zone results in a "bonding" between people they never forget. I repeatedly see strangers begin long-term friendships with people next to them at a meeting where they've slapped their knees, shed a tear, or shared a profound statement made during a speech!

How do you get them elbow to elbow? You can't always. But it's always worth a try.

If the crowd is smaller than planned for and they scatter out, I suggest to the emcee he ask them to "move up front where the swimsuits will be modeled." I may even ask them myself. Certainly, it's easier to move them in a theatre style arrangement, as long as the rows aren't too close. In fact, done early enough (before the salads are attacked) it can also be done by you or the emcee at meal functions.

Occasionally, I speak to high school students. I will typically rearrange the entire crowd if they're not grouped together at the front. It separates "whispering buddies", divides young romantics, and breaks most preoccupations. And it can be done so it's fun for them...like seating tall girls by short boys; seating them by birth month; alternating seniors, juniors, and sophomores; and poking in an occasional teacher. I also do the same for corporate teamwork seminars, because I want them to team up with a "stranger".

HOW TO "MOVE" YOUR AUDIENCE SUCCESSFULLY

Four key ideas I'd encourage you to practice:

First, if you see you're going to "move" your audience, let the meeting planner know. Notice I didn't say ask the meeting planner, I said to "let them know". An insecure meeting planner might say "no" to avoid any inconvenience for the attendees and a negative reflection on themselves. And that might determine if your meeting is a failure or a success. Take control if it will effect the outcome!

Secondly, the more you work the crowd, press the flesh, and introduce yourself one on one before they're seated, the closer they'll crowd up where you need them.

Third, always ask for a long microphone cord or a cordless mike just in case you can't get them moved. You might not have the time or the seating arrangement or the age of the audience might not be conducive to a lot of moving. If the nearest person to you is 30 feet away, for whatever reason, you've got to go to the audience.

Just outside Indianapolis. Annual meeting of a farm lending cooperative. September. Older crowd. Corn Harvest is three weeks early. Normal attendance, 600. Bad news, 300 are still out harvesting corn. The 300 who came sit at the back of the high school auditorium. The first row is 200 feet from the lectern. The President of the organization got no response because he stayed on the stage. (Heck, most of us couldn't even see him). Good news, the janitor has 200 feet of mike cord. After my introduction, I go to the middle of the auditorium, to the first row of people. Awkward, but successful.

Fourth, the more scattered out the group, the more you need to move to the "weighted center" of the group. I have occasionally found it necessary to move to smack dab in the center of a scattered group and speak "in the round", in order to capture their attention and get their response. This practice is especially useful when you get one of those meeting rooms shaped like an "L" or a "T", or when the room has pillars or posts in it that makes it difficult for them to see you.

CHAPTER V

WORKING THE CROWD, PRESSING THE FLESH

– The people you physically touch will think 4 times more highly of you than those you didn't touch.

Minnick's Rule

If I had to pick out one thing that has the greatest influence on audience potential, I'd go immediately to "working the crowd". That's Step 7 in the Audience Potential Index.

And I mean before the speech. In fact, let me share Minnick's Rule *"The more people you can introduce yourself to before your speech, the greater their positive reaction."*

Certainly, there are times when you can't get it done. Maybe there are 1,100 people at a kick off session, the doors open, and they flood in. Obviously, you can't shake hands with all of them. But, you can work the front row or two, introducing yourself and asking their name and hometown. Plus, you can probably work your way up the aisle meeting people in the aisle seats. As you do this, the rest of the audience will see you interacting with others and two things happen. You're suddenly elevated to "celebrity" status, and now they want to hear you more than ever.

I've been amazed at how many meetings I've attended where the speakers made no attempt to meet the head table, much less the audience. If you're Ronald Reagan or Paul Harvey or have similar star status, you probably won't have to "work the crowd". But even if you are Ronald and Paul, I can guarantee it will improve the audience's reaction toward you and your speech.

Another fantastic benefit of working the crowd is the valuable information you pick up about your audience. I never fail to learn less than 5-10 items which can be worked into my speech.

Finally, one of the great fruits of your labor will be the contacts you make for future engagements. How? As you meet people they'll be telling you about meetings coming up or "Did I see you at...?". As an example, I recently spoke to a luncheon of a regional association. As I worked the crowd during their salads, I learned from 3 different sources about a local group that brought in big name speakers every year and had a budget of $5,000.

Salesmen call that prospecting. Plus, people in your audience may refer other meeting planners to you, as well as give you a contact name for other groups. You now have a referral. And everyone knows that a referral is worth 5 times any cold call you'll make.

A LESSON IN FLESH-PRESSING.

First, make sure you've introduced yourself to the meeting planner and the staff as soon as possible. Take the initiative. The staff contact is extremely important. Why? Because they're in the office more than their superior. And when people call in to inquire about your performance, staff members will most likely be the ones responding.

Second, introduce yourself to the head table after they're

seated. Do it from in front. This shows respect to them and creates interest on the part of the audience who are by now pointing to you and asking their tablemates "Is that the speaker?".

Third, meet the Board of Directors—meet every one of them, wives and children. These people are usually leaders in other groups as well, and that means more spin-offs. Plus, their reaction can have a great impact on the meeting planner's opinion of your presentation. If the board likes you, the meeting planner's evaluation will escalate.

TOUCH THE AUDIENCE

How do you work the crowd? Introduce yourself to as many of the audience as you can. If there is a common entrance, stand at the entrance and greet them as they come in. If there is a buffet line, stand in front and greet them, or stand at the front and hand out plates as you greet them.

What do you say? I like to stick out my hand a say, "Howdy, I'm Dale Minnick from Oklahoma, I'm your speaker here today." They'll usually say "Well hello, I'm Jack Doe." If they just say Hi, or nothing, prompt them by saying, "And you are...?"

Some folks will be speechless. Some because they're shy and others because you will have shocked them. Why? Because they've probably never had a speaker introduce themselves. It's unusual and it's very effective.

I like to meet men first then turn to the wife and say "Is this your daughter". There are times you don't use this line. When he's 60 and she's 30, just be courteous and move on. Occasionally, you'll hear "no, she's my grandma", "my live-in", or some similar attempt at cute. That's a great opportunity to have more fun with them, and the laughter you generate will not go unnoticed by the others. They'll be even more excited when you get up to speak.

A few final tips. Don't let your crowd-working interfere with the flow of the meeting. Don't hold up buffet lines, either. Keeping a hungry audience away from food can do more damage than you can heal up with a handshake and a howdy-do.

Be sincere. Ask them about themselves with open-ended who, what, when, where, how, and which questions, and look them in the eyes as you talk and listen. Notice the color of their eyes. Looking at the color of their eyes gives you an even greater appearance of being very sincerely interested in them. You may "feel" sincere, but you've got to show it.

Wherever you are in your speaking career, "working the crowd" will do more for your end result than absolutely any other one thing I've ever found. Plus, it's a great way to organize some of those butterflies and find out in advance that you're going to do a good job.

CHAPTER VI

INTRODUCTIONS: THE KEY OR THE KILLER

– I've been introduced lots of ways and that was certainly one of them.

A "great" introduction can set the tone for a "great" speech. A "good" introduction can still allow a speaker to get up and "show his or her stuff" and turn it into a "great" speech. A "terrible" introduction can raise doubts in the mind of the audience, even your own mind, and force you to work very hard to "get" your audience on your side...and off your back!

Fortunately, you won't get many "terrible" introductions. Unfortunately, you won't get many "great" ones, either. The goal for introduction should be to eliminate all terrible ones and turn more good ones into great ones.

THE "KILLER" INTRODUCTION

Denver, 1979. 10:14 a.m. Mountain Time. I am seated on the front row of a meeting room in a well-known hotel. Behind me are over 100 directors of financial institutions waiting to listen to a wonderful, enchanting economist (me) they'd never ever heard of before. My introducer? A 55 year-old part-time Dale Carnegie instructor, who was also the meeting planner, who was also the emcee, who also prided himself on the fact he memorized introductions and never, never, never, used notes.

I didn't have a written introduction and he didn't need one. He called me a week before the meeting to get my background so he could put a few notes together. He did a rather remarkable job. He accurately depicted my honest rural upbringing, my undergraduate and graduate school education, my manifold civic and professional accomplishments, and my meteoric rise as a corporate economist. He then swept his left hand dramatically toward me, and concluded the introduction with "please give a warm Rocky Mountain welcome to...".

As he paused, you could feel the anticipation build within the audience. They were ready for me, I was ready for them. The pause got longer and longer, and longer. Someone in the audience shifted uncomfortably in his chair. I began to notice some physical changes in my introducer. His pupils were dilated, his smile was gradually disappearing, his arm seemed frozen in space, and a look of horror was quickly taking over his entire body. Then I realized...oh surely not,...could it be,....yes, I do believe,....no doubt about it whatsoever...he had forgotten my name!

WRITTEN INTRODUCTIONS

That experience taught me a valuable lesson. Always have a written introduction, typed and easily read. Send it to the meeting planner along with your "confirmation packet" before the speech and always carry an extra copy with you to the speech as a back-up, just in case.

My first prepared introduction served me well. It was primarily biographical information. And when we needed a biographical sketch instead of an introduction, we simply took off the last line which read "please give a warm welcome to Dale L. Minnick!" What efficiency, an introduction and biographical sketch all in one! Great idea! Wrongggg! Read on!

THE "KILLER" INTRODUCER

July, 1982. Just outside Austin, Texas. Annual meeting of a large cooperative financial group covering 3 rural counties. My introducer? A colorful character who had a local reputation for being an excellent entertaining speaker. I found this out by our conversation before the meeting started. Pleasant chap. Somewhat stand-offish, though.

The first 15 minutes of my introduction, he didn't even mention me. He was "showing his stuff" to the hometown crowd. And doing a pretty good job, too! He finished with flair, received his applause, then announced it was time to introduce the "real speaker". He then slowly and methodically worked his way down my biography with a cutting torch. Gem after gem of sarcastic commentary on my pedigree. When he got through Santa Anna would have been more welcome than me. I learned after the meeting that he thought he should have been hired as their speaker, and was given the job of emcee as a way to try to appease him.

SEPARATING YOUR BIO SHEET AND YOUR INTRODUCTION

After the above experience, I quit using my biographical information for my introduction. The biographical information is designed for my clients' in-house publications, meeting programs, and similar uses. It tells about my background, and why I've earned the right to be their speaker.

My biography for humorous banquet-type speeches is slightly different than for my seminars. And my seminar biography varies slightly to reflect the Sales, Customer Service, Membership Recruitment, or Teamwork emphasis of the seminar. We mail the biography to the meeting planner along with a glossy picture and the rest of our "confirmation packet".

My next great idea was to develop a humorous introduction without the "who cares" biographical information. I wanted to create an introduction that got the emcee a couple of laughs, that got the crowd thinking "funny", and one that created an air of expectancy. Here's my humorous introduction:

> *Our speaker tonight was born and raised on the family's poor homestead near the West Coast of Oklahoma.*

> *His ancestors moved to Oklahoma in a covered wagon.*

> *I've seen some of his old family pictures and I understand why the wagon had to be covered.*

> *Growing up in a big family, he never slept alone until after he got married.*

> *As a member of the National Speakers Association, he's guaranteed to tickle your ribs and put new fire in your heart.*

> *Join me for a great big _____ welcome for Dale Minnick.*

The wording of that introduction makes it especially important that it be read exactly as it's written. I've heard emcees change 3 words and blow the humor into confusion. I like for them to have fun with me, add any cute stories they want, but read the introduction like it's written, please!

We also send the introduction along, plus, I always carry an extra. In 10% of the speeches I do, the meeting planner or the person who's been assigned to introduce me has forgotten or misplaced the introduction. Always, Always, Always carry one with you to the meeting.

KNOW THY INTRODUCER

I always visit with the introducers as much as I can beforehand, often times I'll have him or her fill out a questionnaire about his family, background, achievements, and hobbies. I want us to get to be the best buddies we can be in the shortest amount of time. Plus, I want to reassure him or her that they're going to do a great job.

In many cases the introduction is made by someone who gets up in front of a crowd less frequently than they have a birthday and they're scared to death. Get them to like you, reassure them, get them to expect the laughs they're going to get. Plus, I tell them to have fun with the introduction, but read it like it's written. Then when they get up, they look great, and they make you look great.

Always thank the introducer for the great job they did. If the introducer was obviously nervous and uncomfortable, I like to thank them publicly and follow up with a line like "That was a great job. Last week I was in Texas and I was introduced as an upwind breeze in the cowlot of life!" Find your own funny line and use it. The crowd is relieved, the introducer is relieved, and you've got the crowd under your control.

Have you ever heard an introduction that was done better than the speech? Most speakers would say No! But occasionally I get an introduction that my 11 year-old daughter would say is "awesome". Jack Rucker, Vice-President of the West One Bank in Boise, is an "awesome" introducer. He could introduce the Pope and even get the

Baptists on the edge of their seats. The better the introduction, the more fun you can have with the introducer, and the better your speech will be accepted by your audience.

Always say "Thank You" to the introducer. Three times. When you get up to speak. After your speech. And with a letter after you return home.

Now that you've been introduced, how do you "open" your speech to let your audience see inside? Easy, turn to the next page.

CHAPTER VII

OPENERS — THE FIRST IMPRESSION

– The first few seconds can keep the next few minutes from going on for hours.

Once you've been properly introduced, you're probably going to stick out like a sore thumb if you crawl under your seat. So get up there and go for it.

How you open your speech can very well determine how you finish your speech—either out front accepting applause, or out in back trying to get out the door. Openers should be designed to break the preoccupation of the audience.

Just as salesmen are taught to break the preoccupation of the prospect so that they can get them totally focused on their presentation, so does the speaker need to get his audience to begin focusing on him. I have seen speakers botch their opening, lose their audience, and even have conversation begin to develop that eventually built to the point the speaker was drowned out. This chapter will give you several options to prevent that from ever happening to you.

GET EVEN WITH HUMOR

An opener that acknowledges something in the introduction is very successful. For example, in my introduction I have a list of points that give the introducer a few laughs at my expense. That gives me an opportunity to open with a playful response and perhaps a story or two which makes it look as if I am getting even. It's all set up and it breaks the preoccupation of the audience.

SILENCE

I've seen speakers open with a solid minute of silence, staring at the audience without speaking. As the speaker waits, the audience is initially surprised, followed by great amusement and some laughing, which soon turns into impatience. As the attitude of the crowd begins to border on anger, the speaker begins. His first remarks take a survey of the audience to ask them how many of them experienced the hatred before he began to speak. Then the first point of his presentation deals with controlling your reaction to situations to achieve success.

FORCED LAUGHTER

I've seen humorists begin with 15 seconds of deliberate laughter, either by themselves or along with the audience after inviting them to join. The 15 seconds of laughter (which add an average of 2 days to your life span) is then followed with a discussion about laughter and humor.

THE OUTLANDISH PROMISE

I once observed a very technical speaker begin his presentation with the statement "Before my presentation is over, I am going to have you running up and down the aisle turning furniture over". He then proceeded into his very technical financial services presentation. At the end he recalled his initial remark. He then announced that he had taped three of his business cards to the bottom of three chairs in the room and the first person who brought him one of his cards would be awarded $40, the second one would receive $10, and the third would receive $5. He not only got their attention at the beginning, but no one forgot his presentation the rest of the day and in fact referred to it throughout the day.

IN CHARACTER

Some speakers have had success coming out as an imper-sonator. They are introduced as someone in character and hold that character until a later point in the presentation. While this is a great technique, I also have observed in one out of every four or five audiences, this approach backfires. Some people will not appreciate being duped and it can create resentment that might ruin the ending.

POETRY

Poetry is a great way to open if it is appropriate. Find a favorite or humorous poem that illustrates your opening point and use it immediately after being introduced. Don't acknowledge the introduction, just go to the mike (or have it with you already) and go right into the poem. You can also do the same thing with a fable or self-experience story. Be sure, though, to come "back" to the meeting at some point and thank your introduccer and start acknowledging your audience.

SLAPSTICK

Slapstick can be effective if it is well rehearsed. I remember being introduced once and tripping on the top step and sliding on my tie to the feet of the master of ceremonies. The response was a roar of laughter and approval. Unfortunately, I had tripped over a protruding wire at the top of the steps and my opening was neither intended nor well-rehearsed. (I have not tried it since.)

THE SUBSTITUTE SPEAKER

Some speakers have tried to set the introduction up so that it appears the speaker being introduced is not actually in attendance and the master of ceremonies is in an unfortunate position and needs someone to come up and fill the time. The speaker is then asked by the MC to come up from a table and say a few words.

Other speakers have walked into a room pretending to be a member of the group and asked hostile questions or drawn attention to themselves by yelling and coming into the meeting room as someone in another character, then going into their routine or speech.

CROWD INTERACTION

Crowd interaction is a great way to loosen up the audience. One often-used trick is to instruct the audience to shake hands with the person on their left and watch the reaction that follows. Or ask the audience to introduce themselves to their left and right, instructing them to closely observe the pupils of each others eyes. Following the exercise, inform them that a small or shrinking pupil shows distrust and suspicion—and a large or dilating pupil means that person is physically attracted to you.

Another crowd interaction opener that gets a lot of momentum rolling is to ask each to look at the person on either side of them, then turn back to each and say "You've got the nicest hair I've seen today". Or say "You are the best looking person your age I've ever seen". Remember, though, you must also do whatever you've instructed them to do or they may freeze up and sit there in stone silence. Come up with your own crowd interaction opener, do it with them, and you will win the audience immediately.

Whatever your opener, it should be a preoccupation breaker, and it should fit your style. Many openers that other speakers use successfully are simply not my style. Find one or several that fit your style and use them. There is no limit to the number of ways you can open a speech. The limit is strictly your imagination. Sales people are often taught that you "never get a second chance to make a good first impression" and that your first impression is pretty well sewn up in the first two minutes. Use those two minutes wisely and you'll have a great presentation.

CHAPTER VIII

WRITE A SPEECH IN TWO MINUTES

– You already have a great speech.

WHAT DO YOU SAY?

Communication with an audience requires three basic ingredients: a speaker, which is you; a listener, which is them; and a message, which is...?

What is your message? If your answer to that question is "Well, I'm not really sure", then let me help you with a few simple, easy guidelines.

WHAT TOPICS ARE HOT

As we embark on a new millennium in this service-based economy, topics such as change, leadership, customer service and success will always be at high demand. Personal empowerment or what we used to call motivational speaking, will also continue to be popular.

And you've already got good examples of things that have happened to you in all those areas. And if you can do any or all and do them with a high dose of humor you will have the world knocking on your door.

I highly recommend having a short 5-10 minutes on each one of these topics. Over time you'll be collecting material you'll find to add to each one until you can spend 45 minutes on each topic!

WHAT DOES YOUR AUDIENCE NEED?

Always find out what your audience needs. Every individual and every group has needs, even if they don't think so. The program chairman for the Ladies Club may think her only need is to find somebody to fill the weekly slot. But her group has several needs and you can satisfy those needs by asking some very simple questions.

1. What are the greatest accomplishments of this group?
2. What are the current projects of the group?
3. What are the members' greatest concerns?
4. What are their greatest opportunities?
5. What are their backgrounds and attitudes?
6. What are the most significant things on their minds as they come to the meeting?
7. How much time will I have?
8. Have there been any traumatic happenings to members?
9. What issues are members sensitive about?
10. Who are the leaders and their titles?

I suggest you use both a questionnaire and, occasionally, personal visits before the speech to get these questions answered. Once you have allowed the meeting planner to answer your questions, you can then turn to your own personal experiences to start building your speech.

ORGANIZING YOUR SPEECH

One of the best suggestions I could give to help you organize your speech is simple. Very simple. Take your first name and build your speech using a theme which starts with each letter. For example Dale might become Dedication, Attitude, Loyalty, and Enthusiasm. I could then build 10 minutes on each one and I'd have a full-length keynote. Here's some alphabetical ideas to fit into your name and get you started:

Attitude or Action	Natural
Boldness	Opportunities
Commitment or Courage	Peace, Procrastination
Dedication	Quiet
Enthusiasm	Responsibility
Family	Success
Give	Talent
Happiness	Understanding
Implement or Initiate	Visualization
Joy	Wisdom
Kindness	Xenomorphic
Laughter or Loyalty	You
Mission	Zeal

If your name is Al or Ed, your speech may be too short. You will want to use your real name or add your middle name. If your name is Englebert Humperdink, you may want to just sing instead of speaking. The greatest benefit of this method is that if you ever "freeze up" in front of an audience you won't forget where you're going. That is, unless you forget your name, in which case I'd suggest faking a heart attack!

MIND-MAPPING

Another way to organize your speech is to use mind-mapping. Mind-mapping involves simply drawing a circle in the middle of a sheet of paper. In the middle of the circle write your "focus" topic, your main point. Then use lines out from the circle to write your major points and minor points.

RECALL YOUR PERSONAL EXPERIENCES

The greatest asset you can bring to a speaking assignment is your personal experience. You have had many, many, triumphs and many, many, trials that tie in with the needs of your audiences. Recall those personal experiences. Reconstruct them. Present them skillfully. You'll have the audience in your pocket.

One of the best pieces of advice I ever received was from a speaker who said "...the first thing you ought to do when you decide you're going to be a speaker is to take two weeks off, go to the Bahamas, get some paper and a pen, sit on the beach, and start writing down your life experiences."

You may not have two weeks to take off and go to the Bahamas, so let me give you a shorter method. Below I've selected 24 time periods in your life. The significance of these time periods is that everyone in your audiences will identify with these time periods, too.

Now get ready to do some thinking, some fun thinking. Start with No. 1 "Birth to Kindergarten" and beside each write down the most significant things that happened to you during each time period. Write down the good, the bad, the ugly, and the pretty things that happened. Use only a word or two to remind you of the situation. Spend one minute on each period. I'll be timing you. Ready? Set? Go!

WHAT HAPPENED DURING
THESE PERIODS OF YOUR LIFE?

1. Birth to Kindergarten _____

_____

2. 1st, 2nd & 3rd Grade Years _____

_____

3. 4th, 5th, & 6th Grade Years _____

_____

4. 7th, 8th, & 9th Grade Years (Jr Hi) _____

_____

5. 10th, 11th & 12th Grade Years (HighSch) _____

_____

6. College _____

_____

7. Dating _____

_____

8. Marriage _____

_____

9. Work Life _____

_____

10. Husbands and Wives _____

_____

11. Having and Raising Children _____

_____

12. Hobbies and Sports I've Enjoyed _____

_____

13. My Church Life _____

_____

14. Strange People I Have Known _____

_____

15. My Health and Medical Experiences _____

_____

16. Pets and Animals I Have Owned and Known _____

_____

17. Divorces I Have Known About _____

_____

18. My Most Embarrassing Moment _____

_____

19. My Most Painful Experience_____

_____

20. My Travelling Experiences _____

_____

21. My Greatest Success _____

_____

22. My Worst Failure _____

_____

23. Places I've Lived _____

_____

24. Death (other than speaking) _____

_____

Okay, time's up. Put down your pencil and hand in your answers (Just kidding). Most people find it's difficult to spend only one minute on each because one memory leads to another, then another, then still another. However, in less than 30 minutes you have developed a tremendous list of personal experiences from which you can choose pertinent examples to address the needs and interests of your audience. Your audience will be interested because hearing your personal experiences will trigger memories of their own.

Don't be afraid to borrow from others' experiences — a wise old sage once said "If you want to be successful, learn from others' mistakes. You won't have time to make'em all yourself." Use stories and experiences from family, friends, co-workers, and others. Go back for just a moment to your list of personal experiences and think about personal experiences of others that fit into each time period. Incorporate them into your speech and you'll add variety and another perspective.

Now that you've got your personal experience stories, and organized your speech by using your first name or mind-mapping, you're ready for the next step. Incorporate humor into your presentation and you'll get everyone cheering you on with laughter.

CHAPTER IX

STAND AND DELIVER

– Drive on, drive on and never let 'em see you sweat.

Go into your presentation with courage. There's genius in boldness. Everyone respects a man or woman with courage. Even horses. Approach a horse timidly with your knees shaking and he'll buck, snort, shy, and kick. So will your audience. Approach a horse with courage and he'll follow your every cue and command. So will your audience.

It's important to remember that the words you use in your speech will account for only about 7% of your success with the audience. Approximately 38% of your success will result from your voice. The remaining 55%, or over half of your success will result from your body language and gestures.

THE VOICE

Before you arrive at the speech make sure your voice is loosened up. Say the words "keep calm" in sing-song fashion over and over, each time a note lower than before until you get as low as you can go. Doing it with a piano helps when time and location permit. Repeating this exercise over time can also lower your natural speaking voice.

Don't drink milk products or eat syrupy, sugary foods before you speak. They'll cause you to keep clearing your throat to get rid of that "coating" on your vocal chords. Some speakers like cold drinks before they speak, I prefer warm water. Hot coffee is not very good but I prefer it when the only other option is ice cold.

There will be times when your voice isn't up to par due to a cold or flu. I remember a speech in 1989 at the Broadmoor in Colorado Springs. I flew in and picked up my rental car in total silence — a few hoarse sounds were all I could make. I walked into the hotel and a miracle occurred. My voice came back for the next two hours. The speech went well. I left the hotel and my voice left me.

For those occasions when your voice is iffy because of a cold, flu, or fatigue, I suggest a natural health food, Echinacea. It's a great temporary cure. You can make a warm tea with it, or mix it with something else (whiskey is not recommended).

Now use that voice to advantage. Use it high, use it low. Notice how newsman Paul Harvey uses that technique. Change the speed of your speech from slow to fast and back to slow. Draw out the vowels. Listen to Zig Ziglar as he drags out the vowels on the last word of the sentences to make his point.

If you're good at impressions, imitations, and dialects, use them. If you're not, don't. Experiment with accents to add life to your characters and your stories. Take a close look at your material to see what stories you could beef up with an added voice.

GESTURES

My greatest advice for gestures is to use them! And

remember, the bigger the audience, the bigger the gesture —
that helps the people in back get the same "feel" of your
gestures as those in front.

For example in humorous anecdote number 61 as I say the
words "The brides veil" my left hand goes toward the back
of my head, then I say "went all the way down to the cuff...on
her overalls" my hand moves to my cuff and I lean over. Look
at your materials and see where you can add gestures.

Gestures should always complement your message. Have
you ever been distracted by someone talking nervously and
throwing their hands all around? Naturally, you start
watching their hands and stop listening to the words. One
humorist I know positions himself sideways to the center of
the audience as he approaches his punchline, then delivers
his punch line over his shoulder for greater emphasis and
results.

If you're describing a conversation between two people, look
in a different direction or move from one imaginary side to
the other for each character's words. Fall on the floor like
Ed Foreman or get down on one knee like Zig. They use
those gestures because they work.

NOTES

If you're not totally comfortable with your speech, care
enough about your audience to use notes. And if you lose
your place, relax, find it again, and don't worry about the
pause. In fact, "planned pauses" are very effective. Even an
"unplanned pause" can be effective if you handle it well.

I gave my first speech when I was 14. I wrote it, typed it out,
stood behind the lectern, and escaped unhurt, with little eye
contact. Most professional speakers I know started like I
did, with a memorized speech and a full set of typewritten

notes as a crutch. I still recommend a full set of notes for new speakers, as well as for old speakers with a brand new speech.

After a few times, you'll get comfortable with more eye contact, more gestures, more voice fluctuations, and fewer notes. You may then go to idea cards as your crutch. Former President George Bush used 5" X 7" cards very effectively. His main ideas and supporting statements were typed on the cards. His lectern, which traveled with him, had a sliding bar in the middle to hold his cards. As he finished each he pulled it to the side. He also had cues on his cards for when to emphasize words, when to pound on the lectern, and when to turn to someone else on the platform to acknowledge them.

Once you get really comfortable with your speech you may want to go to the summary sheet. This is what I use. Before my speech, I list the stories I'm going to use, in proper order; and I perform mentally the special gestures or punch lines. Then I put it in my pocket or back in the client file out of sight. That summary has now been etched in my subconscious in almost miraculous fashion. As I finish one story, the next one pops up as if by magic. Plus, when I'm finished I review the summary sheet and add other stories I included, delete those I didn't, write the names of my audience participants, and when I'm invited back, I don't use the same material.

LECTERNS

First, let me make you aware that most people use the terms "lectern" and "podium" interchangeably. To use a church example, the lectern is analogous to the pulpit. The word "podium" most appropriately describes a riser or low stage.

Whatever you call it, the lectern is important. It declares the focal point of a meeting room. The President of the United

States takes his own with him wherever he goes. It's called the "Blue Goose" and it's adjustable in height, has three microphones on the top, it's padded (so he can pound on it for emphasis), and it contains a bullet proof shield. I had the pleasure of sharing the platform with the President once. The Secret Service man informed me if anyone started shooting while I was speaking to drop behind the podium. I asked him if he thought the President was in danger? He said no, but he'd heard me speak before.

Early in my career I loved lecterns. I leaned on them, hid behind them, rested my notes on them, and occasionally held on to them for dear life. One night in Haxtun, Colorado at the high school auditorium, their beautiful lectern was placed upstage (away from the audience) more than I realized until I went on stage. Too far from the crowd, I took the mike out of the holder and went to the very front lip of the stage. The freedom was so great and the audience response so wonderful, I have never used a lectern since unless absolutely forced.

HAND PROPS

One of my former college professors used to carry a pistol into the room at test time, set it on the lectern and inform the class there would be no cheating or talking. It was very effective.

Props can add a lot to your effectiveness because they add to the picture you're painting in the minds of those in the audience. One fellow speaker uses a cowbell he rings whenever he makes a point he wants them to remember. Others use magic tricks, slides, videos, overheads, and even live animals.

I have a cowboy poem I wrote years ago about chickens. For years, I always had the meeting planner furnish a chicken (I quit carrying my own — you'd be surprised at the strange looks you get checking into a hotel late at night with a chicken under your arm).

At a certain place in the poem the chicken was to be launched from offstage. Over the years I've had some great birds, too. The black show bird in Albuquerque that landed in the french dressing, then crowed each time the audience laughed...the matronly hen in Nebraska who laid a soft shell egg on the head table...and many who, in their fright, made a statement on the carpet, the table cloth, and, occasionally, a salad plate.

I also use hats in my speeches. In my seminars I use a stethoscope, balls of twine, "come alive" overheads, money, door prizes, and even the microphone. Look at your material and see where a prop here or there would add to its effect. And have fun!

AUDIENCE PARTICIPATION

I always use some form of audience participation. I will use 3 or 4 people out of the audience during my speech to help me with a story, or cowboy poem. For that reason, and to be able to get into the crowd, I always request a hand held microphone with a long cord.

Some speakers are horrified at the thought of using participants, particularly in humorous skits where they might be embarrassed. But because I work the crowd heavily and know the audience well, I've never had one complaint.

Plus, I always get the proper names and addresses of the "volunteers" from the meeting planner (who recommended them to me in the first place) and send them a letter of appreciation after I return to my office.

CLOSINGS

The words you use in the final 30 seconds may well be the

ones your audience remembers most. They can be funny, serious, or poetic, but they should always be memorable.

I've tried all different kinds of closings and have had success with all of them. A friend of mine has 3 closings — a short one, an intermediate one, and a long one. If his time has been cut, he goes with the short closing. If the crowd is really with him, he'll use the long closing.

Summary closes can be effective when you briefly in one sentence review the points you've made, then finish with a "clincher".

One speaker I know starts a story early on in his speech, and then gets sidetracked and at the last minute "suddenly" remembers he didn't finish his story. He finishes it with flare and that's his closing.

Another speaker I know just gets to the end and says "I've enjoyed being with you, Thank you very much" and he's done. He gets by with this because he has already painted a picture in their minds of coming up to him afterwards and saying a "secret" word to show their pleasure.

Two final ideas about your delivery. When you close and the applause begins, remember you can draw the applause out longer by turning from side to side and saying "Thank You, Thank You, Thank You very much". The audience will keep applauding just about as long as you keep saying "Thank you" and bowing humbly.

Finally, the words of Doc Blakely, well-known humorist, still ring in my ears. He said, "Dale, to be a success in this business you don't have to be great every time, but do be consistently good". Those words have rung so true. I can't always get a standing ovation or 10 spin-off bookings at the conclusion of every speech, but I can do my very best at each one.

CHAPTER X

EXPECTING THE UNEXPECTED

– Planning for the accidents will make you a hero.

"That would never happen to me." Ever heard someone say that about a wild unexpected event during someone's presentation? Or have you ever said it yourself? Just for starters let me give you three real-life incidents and you think about how you'd handle them.

UNEXPECTED INCIDENT NO. 1

Springfield, Illinois. Late April. 350 state leaders. Two tiered head table. Group President is retiring after 30 years. The big finale—me! I'm eloquently introduced. I move down in front with a cordless mike. Four minutes into the program the mike starts buzzing and crackling and people in the back start shouting "can't hear". What would you do?

I recover, 30 minutes into the presentation. Really on a roll. A rock and roll band on the other side of the folding wall starts their first set for the Junior Prom. (As loud as it was, I think they were also playing for a Junior Prom in Indiana.) What would you do?

UNEXPECTED INCIDENT NO. 2

Outside Des Moines. September. Unusually hot. Unusu-

humid. Unusually windy. Outdoor meeting. 3,000 people under a huge tent. Older group. Three people already fainted. I'm introduced. Great crowd. Thirty-two minutes into my speech. On a roll in the middle of one of my best stories. Wind whips tent off a tent pole. Pole is 20 feet long, 5 inches across. Comes down in the crowd. Chairs turn over, people falling. Screaming. Someone shouts "Call an ambulance". Several people down. A cry for wet towels to wipe up blood. What would you do?

UNEXPECTED INCIDENT NO. 3

North Little Rock. 200 local managers from 4 states. Corporate meeting. Long cocktail hour. One manager, his name is "Gator" (really), from Louisiana spent two hours at cocktail hour. He's ready for the speaker. I'm introduced. Takes longer than usual. Gator is making comments. I start to speak. Gator screams, "We don't want to hear a speaker, we want to go get drunk!" What would you do?

RESPONDING TO INCIDENT NO. 1

Two problems here. First, the mike problem. Not an uncommon occurrence. In this case I apologized to the audience, blamed it on the Russians, and moved back to the fixed lectern microphone. I then thanked those who told me they couldn't hear, blamed it on the Russians again and continued, with some minor alterations to my speech due to my lack of mobility.

Some mike problems are not easily remedied. I have had to stand on a chair and finish my speech when the sound system died an untimely death. As we discovered in Chapter 4, thoroughly checking the room set-up and equipment well before your presentation can prevent some equipment difficulties, but always be prepared for the unexpected.

Now the rock and roll band. I always ask what other meetings are on in adjacent rooms. I learned to ask, after having been forced into competition with a life-threatening bass guitar a few times. In most cases, the meeting planner will get the band shut down.

Keep in mind though, while the meeting planner is finding the right authority to get the band to quit, you're still going to have to deal with 4-5 minutes of loud music. You obviously can't sit down and finish your dessert, so what do you do?

Always, always drive on!

I usually get tickled myself or at least act tickled when something like this happens and, watching my laughter, the audience soon follows. (Remember, the audience will get its cue from you). Plus, I have lines "in my pocket" for these occasions. They look like ad libs to the audience, which they should, and can turn the situation from a horror into a highlight.

However you react, if you drive on, the audience's sympathy for you and anger against the source of interruption will grow. Plus, if you'll get the audience to give the rock and roll band a hard time when they quit it'll give everyone a boost...especially the meeting planner who's facing a hostile crowd across the wall. Finally, when the meeting planner comes back into the room, get her/him another round of applause and follow with another "out of pocket" ad lib, and continue on with your speech.

Now let me walk you through a hypothetical situation with a rock and roll band next door and the steps you might take.

Step 1. Band starts up.

Step 2. Keep your sense of humor.

Step 3. Use ad libs. Here are some ideas:

> Turn to chairman and say "Sam, I think your hearing aid is on the blink...Can you get the ball game on that thing?

Or, in the right group—get the emcee and his wife up to dance and get the audience on their feet to dance and clap to the music.

Or, "Nothing like good music...and that's nothing like good music."

Or, turn to chairman and say, "Bill, I think you left the radio on in your car."

Or, "They tell me that's what a SCUD Missile sounds like."

Step 4. Music quits, "Let's give that band a hand to show our appreciation."

Step 5. Continue with your speech.

Step 6. Meeting planner returns. Ask for a standing ovation. After it dies down, ask her/him if you need to call an ambulance for anybody over there?

Step 7. Continue your speech.

Step 8. If you tell a dud story later (you can even plant a dud) follow up with a Johnny Carson type "Where's that band when I need them."

RESPONDING TO INCIDENT NO. 2

The tragic tent pole incident. If you speak very many years you will encounter an unfortunate event like this. It may be someone who has collapsed. I've known speakers who've had deaths occur during their speech. Here's what I did.

Step 1. Acknowledge the accident. The group was so large many hadn't noticed. Those who had were panicking. I said "Ladies and Gentlemen, we've had an accident in the audience here (I pointed where). I'm going to ask those of you who are not injured to please be seated unless you're helping someone. Please be seated. Thank you.

Step 2. Asked everyone to please stay in their seats to give the victims air and helpers room to work.

Step 3. Diverted their attention by asking them to bow and pray quietly for those who may be hurt.

Step 4. Asked for any nurses or doctors to please make themselves known to someone on stage.

Step 5. Relayed instructions over the microphone to call for an ambulance and made sure someone was responding and informed the group that the ambulance had been called.

Step 6. Relayed a request over the microphone for wet towels.

Step 7. When the excitement had begun to subside and the crowd was under control, I turned the mike back to the chairman of the board who was the emcee and suggested quietly to the President that he have some people quickly and discreetly check the safety of the tent.

Initially, when the accident occurred, it appeared that as many as 50-100 people had been injured, judging from the turmoil in the audience. When it was all finished, only one man was seriously injured and taken to the hospital unconscious.

Okay, now, the excitement is over, the tragedy is behind you and the emcee is about to bring you back on. How do you get the crowd back?

If you're a humorist, you have to move back into your humor slowly. Shift to something in you repertoire that will tie into the event and yet break their preoccupation. I personally believe it is the speaker's responsibility to bring the crowd back "up" and leave them as "up" as you possibly can.

Fortunately, in my tent pole incident, I was spared. The tent was determined to be unsafe, and the remainder of the program was cancelled. Except for the door prizes. A lot of people had come because of the great door prizes. So they moved to the perimeter of the tent while two brave employees stood on stage and announced the winners. I went to the exit and stood there shaking as many hands and thanking as many people as possible for coming.

I wanted the audience to be "cheered up" as they left. Surprisingly, as I shook their hands and said thank you and good-bye, the most common question asked was not "How bad was that fella hurt" or "Is he OK". The most common question was "How'd that story end?"

When I got home I sent a written copy of that story to the meeting planner to publish in their monthly newspaper, 'cause they'd had several phone calls asking the same question "How'd that story end?" I also sent the injured man a get well card and a free cassette tape. He recovered anyway!

RESPONDING TO INCIDENT NO. 3

The Heckler. The very foremost rule to remember in regard to Hecklers is: Don't respond too soon.

While the heckler may be annoying you, it's important to wait until the crowd is also annoyed and on your side. Then you can say something. Keep it brief.

The great humorist Senator Bob Murphy from Nacogdoches, Texas, told me he had responded to a heckler by stopping, pausing, and saying "Ya know I had a fellow last week trying to do what you're doing...." Pause. "...embarrassed him pretty bad in front of everybody..." Pause. "....and I was pretty hard on him...." Pause. "...Then I found out later he was mentally retarded...." Pause. "...So I'm not gonna say anything to you." He waited for the laughter to subside and continued with his speech unheckled.

In my case, I got off a lot easier by another approach. My approach was to start including Gator in my speech. I used him in a couple of my stories. He got what he wanted — attention. And I got what I wanted — some big laughs. He finally shut up and let me finish in peace.

I also was prepared for Gator, because I had done a good job working the crowd. During my flesh pressing I heard about Gator and his reputation of getting inebriated and intimidating the banquet speaker.

I even hunted Gator up and introduced myself. I thought that might stop him, but he'd had too much to drink. However, having met him made it a lot easier to have fun with him and work it to my advantage.

ALWAYS BE PREPARED

The keys to handling "shocks" during a speech are to be prepared, don't give up, keep driving on, and stay relaxed. If you'll stay relaxed and keep your sense of humor, your creative mind will come up with the solution you need.

In 1982, I was asked to speak to a parent-child banquet for a high school group at the small school I graduated from. Just before I was introduced, I went to the bathroom. During my trip, the zipper on my pants broke, and I was both aghast and a-gaping! Plus I had to walk out past the group and I'd already noticed there was no lectern to stand behind.

I panicked for a while. I couldn't take my coat off and tie it around my waist backwards — everyone would know my problem. I couldn't very well walk out like a Mickey Mouse watch — with both hands at 6:30! — they would really know, then.

After I relaxed and got my sense of humor back, I realized I could button the bottom button on my sports coat; put my left hand in my left pocket; twist my coat around just a little and keep my coat tail close to my problem — and no one could tell.

I walked out, I was introduced, I used only one-armed gestures, left with my notes under my left arm and shook hands with my right hand.

Be prepared, be persistent, be relaxed and have fun.

CHAPTER XI

WHAT TIME DOES THE NOON STAGE LEAVE

– Don't be a road-weary speaker, become a road warrior.

"I would just love to travel and visit all those exciting places you see!" I wish I had a dollar for each time I've heard that.

Travel can be exciting and fun...much of the time. It can also be frustrating, time-consuming, lonely, and at times, very boring.

FLYING THE BIG BIRDS

"This is your captain speaking, we are now number one for take off..." What he didn't say was this is the third time we've been down the runway and we haven't been off the runway yet. True story. We had already been down the runway twice without leaving the planet — and we'd unloaded twice while they worked on the plane. Third time's a charm, good-bye Kansas City International.

All the major airlines have names you probably don't know about.

American = *A Miracle Everyone Isn't Convulsive And Nauseous*
United = *Ugly Nerds In Transit Every Day*
USAIR = *You Stay And I Ride*
TWA = *Travel With Anxiety*
Delta = *Don't Ever Leave The Airport*

As much as I like to poke fun at the airlines, they're still great when you compare them with airlines in other countries. I've flown China Air from Beijing to Hong Kong and you haven't lived till you've waited in a Communist line for 3 hours while they wait for the plane to fill up. Ditto for Aeroflot flight from Tblisi, Georgia, USSR to Moscow, where the guy next to me had a box full of chickens on his lap. Even bad service here is better than good service there.

Airlines and airports can be great sources of humor material...and great sources of embarrassment. 1982. I'm headed to Nashville for a speech and I'm running late. My ticket's in my suitcase. I set the suitcase up on the ticket counter, open it, and get out the ticket. The agent sees the ticket and says "You can just barely make it if you run to Gate C4." I slam the suitcase shut, pull it off the counter to head to C4. I forgot one small detail...I forgot to shut the clasps on the suitcase! As I turned and pulled the suitcase off the counter, it opened...and every item neatly packed inside shot out like marbles and fanned out in a huge semicircle across the shining airport floor. Oh, look, there's my razor over by American. My socks rolled into the revolving door...and strangers from all around the world were picking up my underwear and bringing it to me with guarded looks on their faces. I wanted to crawl in the suitcase myself!

Needless to say, I missed my flight and the ticket agent at the Oklahoma City airport still refers to me as Hanes, Size 34 when I walk up.

Let me try to give you some flying tips that will help. First, the basics. Get a good travel agent who has a good computer reservation system and knows how to use it.

Get the best deal you can for your client. Fares are the cheapest for stays over Saturday night. Occasionally, when I have a weekday speech and the fare is extremely high, my agent saves me money by getting two roundtrip tickets with Saturday nights stays and "legs" me in cheaper than one round trip.

Advance fares (3-day, 7-day, 14-day, 21-day depending on the airline) are also cheaper. However, they're not usually refundable. If you book an advance airline reservation in solid, then get another engagement and want to include it in the same trip, you will likely have difficulty changing your advance purchase without some added money.

Frequent flyer miles are useful. If you fly a lot, get signed up with every major airline. Some speakers try to fly with one airline as much as possible to accumulate frequent flyer mileage. I don't. I always look for the best deal for my client. Unfortunately, that means I build up a few frequent flyer miles on a lot of different airlines. Some require more than others to qualify for free tickets and upgrades.

I use frequent flyer miles to off-set travel expenses. Occasionally I use them when a client has little or no funds for my travels. In cases where travel exceeds 40% of my fee, I'll use frequent flyer coupons to reduce those expenses. Plus, it allows me to turn some of those frequent flyer miles into cash.

Have a back-up flight in mind. When my staff makes reservations for me, we always make sure we have a back-up flight. In other words, we don't book the very last flight out if we can avoid it. Sometimes speaking engagements are so close together there's only one choice, but we always try to leave room to make an alternative flight in case of delays or cancellations. Have a back-up flight in mind whenever possible. Flights will be cancelled.

One evening in 1989, I was trying to leave Saginaw, Michigan, for Chicago and was fogged in. All flights were cancelled. I, and another speaker on the program, rented a station wagon and found four other people to join us. One college professor, two speakers, an airline stewardess, a tugboat mechanic and an 18-year-old girl who was missing her engagement party in North Carolina (she cried all the way from Saginaw to Chicago, about 8 hours). What a group. The college professor made a wrong turn and headed us to Detroit. We drove 100 miles before we realized the back window was down and all the luggage in the back — including my briefcase with my check in it — got rain soaked and almost fell out!

When flights get cancelled, I don't stand in line to let them re-route me. I go to the telephone and call my travel agent, or if it's after hours, I call the 1-800 number for my airline and get new reservations. It's much faster and a lot less frustrating.

If you lose a ticket, don't panic. I left a ticket in a hotel room 3 hours from Minneapolis just a few months ago. I didn't realize my problem until I got to the airport. The airline wrote me a new one-way ticket for $50, which was refunded when I sent in the misplaced ticket. If I had been using a frequent flyer ticket, the cost would have been more, but also refunded when I sent in the new one. Most airlines have this same policy. A few regional airlines don't and losing a ticket is your tough luck.

Remember that many flights overbook. That is, they have more reservations than they have seats. They know that not everyone's going to show up. To avoid getting an undesirable seat (which is a window or center seat for me) have your travel agent get your seat assignment in advance. A few airlines have "open" seating which means "first come gets first seat choice".

In the case of the most overbooked flights, once all the seats are taken, they'll first ask if anyone's willing to give up their seat for nothing and take another flight. If there are no takers, the auction begins. They'll start at $100 and go up. I've seen as high as $400 paid for someone to give up their seat. It's usually paid in credit vouchers and is usually in addition to a seat on another flight. Don't jump at the first offer. Normally, I'm trying to get to my destination and have only once accepted a later flight and a credit voucher.

Finally, never check luggage. You should always use carry-on bags for several reasons, but primarily because you may just need your things when you get there. You may not know this, but airlines don't even allow their own pilots and stewardess to check their luggage. They know it might get lost! If you need the contents of your bag, don't check it!

A friend says you can tell you've got problems when you go to report lost luggage, and the guy behind the counter has your clothes on! If you do need to check a bag (sometimes I'm carrying handout materials, etc. in a bag) always carry a separate carry-on with enough clothes to get you by (and an original of your handout) for the first meeting.

FLYING IN SMALL PLANES

I went through a period of my life when I avoided commercial airlines at every opportunity. If I had to fly, I used a charter service with a single-engine plane. In fact, I got so paranoid and claustrophobic about flying commercially, I pictured myself trapped in a metal tube being hurled through space like an Iraqi Missile, just looking for a place to blow up!

My aversion to commercial flying lasted about 3 months. It ended one Saturday morning on the end of a runway in the Panhandle of Oklahoma. The time was 8:32 a.m. and I was ready to head west across the Rockies to Cortez, Colorado for a luncheon speech.

For the previous 36 hours a "small" plane had been causing me lots of problems. I had been stranded all night in an abandoned terminal at a small airport outside Kansas City. A storm had rolled in during my evening speech and we were "weathered in" until about 3:00 a.m. When the pilot finally got the "All Clear" from flight service, he discovered he'd left the key on and we had no batteries. We "prop-started" the plane by hand and got it started, but had no instrument lights. Our only choice was to wait until daybreak. We found two old chairs to sleep in, and at daybreak we prop-started the plane again and got in the air.

We flew about 30 minutes without instruments and decided to land and find a mechanic. Besides, my pilot said he had enough problems flying without a license! I had another speech that next evening outside Amarillo, Texas and we barely made it because of additional delays to stop and check out the electrical system.

So here we are, almost ready to head across the Rockies, a beautiful day. I'd gotten a little sleep after my Amarillo speech. I was looking forward to flying across the mountains, speaking, then flying home to spend Saturday night with my family.

But wait. As the charter pilot does his run up checklist, he notices the plane is running rough...rougher! We're blocking another plane that's ready for take-off. Suddenly, the blocked pilot keys his microphone and screams "Hey 103 Papa, your plane's on fire!"

No sooner had the word "fire!" come over the radio, when I

noticed the paint on the "hood" in front of the windshield was beginning to blister up from the heat of the flames in the engine compartment. There was only one door on the airplane—and it was on my side. I don't remember opening the door, grabbing my briefcase, or unfolding out of my seat. One moment I was in, next moment I was out!

Fortunately, we were on the ground when it happened, we got out alive, and yes, I saved my speech. Another few seconds, though, and I would have been flying over the Rockies without a plane. Unbelievably, I also made it to my speech! I found another pilot with an airplane with two engines that weren't on fire. We took off two hours late. I walked into the meeting room just in time to hear my own introduction (the meeting planner assumed I was already there), walked right to the microphone, and had a wonderful time (it's amazing how much better you speak after almost losing your life.)

HOTELS

I learned a long time ago that getting a good night's rest can have a lot to do with being successful in front of an audience. Unless you sleep well standing up, or folded up, hotels become very important.

I've stayed in many great hotels. I've also been in some I'd like to forget. Like the one in Reserve, New Mexico about 5 hours from Alburqurque. Drove in late. Sunday night. Only one hotel. No one there, not even the manager. Went next door to the bar and met a young cowboy who knew where the manager was — up in the mountains about 2 miles away. The young cowboy would be glad to take me up there in a few minutes. Right after the fight in the parking lot, which he started! He got whipped! Then he took me to the hotel manager, who was in a friend's trailer, smoking his socks or something that smelled as bad. I got into the room at 2:00 a.m., just about the time the hot water tank broke!

A friend said he stayed in a hotel that was so bad the "Do Not Disturb" sign was around the maid's neck. He said he discovered a rat in his room and called the front desk. They sent up another pillow!

One speaker said he stayed in a great hotel out in West Texas. It wasn't fancy, and after his speech he went to bed, but there was a lot of partying going on. About 1 o'clock in the morning the sheriff knocked on his door and asked "Do you have a woman in there?" My friend said "No, sir!" The sheriff opened the door and threw one in!

Seriously, I've had some strange experiences with hotels. Like the night I got into Albuqurque, checked in, went to my room, turned the key, and opened the door to find a very surprised and somewhat angry couple staring back at me. I excused myself and went back to the front desk to get an unoccupied room.

A prominent female speaker I know checked into a New York hotel and as she got ready for bed noticed there was something very strange about the mirror above the dresser. She finally convinced the manager to investigate. He found that an assistant manager had installed a one-way mirror in the room. The adjoining room contained video equipment. The assistant manager would put prominent guests in the room, send up a prostitute, then film the encounter and "blackmail" the guest! True Story! My friend got profuse apologies and a new room. The assistant manager got a new job — probably in Hollywood.

I prefer non-smoking rooms in a quiet area of the hotel. And I'm not afraid to ask for a better room if I'm not pleased.

Always ask for the commercial rate if you haven't made previous arrangements, it can save you and your client lots of money.

If I'm staying more than one night I like to leave a note of thanks and a tip for the chambermaid. After all a tip is supposed to be an advance payment "To Insure Performance" and it usually pays dividends in good service.

A speaker friend of mine likes to have fun with the maids when he's staying in the same room several nights. He takes the paper "cleanliness seal" off the toilet seat every night and puts it back every morning when he leaves the room. After two or three days, all the maids will be talking about him!

The president of a corporation I once worked in gave me one additional suggestion. When he got into a favorite hotel late at night, where he had made no previous reservations, and found they had no vacancies, he would say, "I don't understand, my secretary always makes my reservations and this is where we always stay!" He wasn't lying because both were true. He usually got a room.

Another old trick when encountering a "No Vacancy" situation is to ask them if the President of the United States were to drop in, would you find him a room? The desk clerk will say "Of course". Then say "Well he's not coming, so give it to me!"

RENTING A CAR

Renting a car sounds like a simple task—so why even discuss it? I've been shocked at the number of people I've worked with who have never rented a car in their life. Some are even corporate types. They've always had someone pick them up when they flew into a city. Whether you've rented a car or not, you'll be interested in this segment.

Which company should you use? Go for the best deal you can find! My travel agent is the best source for me. She can pull up all the options, find any special offers, and give me the choices.

I do have a "corporate rate" card with one specific company.

Pick a major company and apply for one. The major benefit I've found is not the daily fee, but the unlimited mileage allowed. Some car rental companies allow only 60 or 80 free miles. My "corporate rate" card usually allows me to get unlimited mileage. I use the word "usually" because I've found that car rental outlets in some cities are independently owned. They may carry the name of the major company, but they don't always offer the same incentive programs.

Rental cars come in luxury, full size, mid size, economy, compact, or "bread box" size. I prefer to rent full size or luxury cars because I'm tall and I don't fold well for long periods of time. Plus, often times, the "weekend rates" and specials for luxury cars are less than the rates for smaller cars.

Even when you're not flying, it may be cheaper for your client if you rent a car rather than drive your personal car. Let me explain. Let's say you've got a speech 500 miles away that is not easily accessible by air. Rent a luxury car with unlimited mileage. Drive to your speech in style, drive back in style. You may save money for your client. For example, I bill mileage expense at the IRS rate, currently 27.5 cents per mile. If I drove my car 1000 miles to a speech and back, I'd bill the client for mileage expense of $275. However, if I can rent a car for, let's say $50 a day and I take three days to make the round trip, that's $150. Add to that $60 for gas (1000 miles at 20 miles per gallon costing $1.20 per gallon). His total cost is $210. I've saved my client money as well as wear and tear on my own car, plus I've ridden in a luxury car probably better than my own.

Consider not buying the insurance coverage when you rent. Here's how to avoid it. First, check with your insurance agent. Your present coverage may protect you when you rent a car. Secondly, some credit cards offer car rental insurance if you bill the reservation to your card number. I carry a Gold American Express card that offers comprehensive and medical coverage when I rent a car. Call your credit card company and find out how to get the service and check the details about how much coverage they offer.

Always take your driver's license with you. I'm getting pretty basic, right? Could be, but let me share a story. One Tuesday night in 1990, I was stopped at a security check in our family car. After passing through, I laid my license on the dash. Next day, I drove to the airport in a different vehicle, flew to St. Louis and attempted to pick up my reserved car. "May I please see your driver's license and a major credit card." Familiar statement. They all ask it. Guess where my license was?

Here I am. Four hours from the resort where I'm speaking in 4 1/2 hours (the plane was 3 hours late, too). No shuttle to the resort till the next morning. I tried complimenting the rental agent on the beautiful earring, but "he" wasn't impressed. I finally came up with a great idea. All he needed was the driver's license number, and to verify it was valid I called the Oklahoma Highway Patrol District office in my home area. Great idea!

It's Saturday, only a dispatcher and a lieutenant are on duty and they can't give out that information anyway. Fortunately, I convinced the lieutenant who I was by telling him everything on my driving record since I was 12. He finally agreed to confirm to the desk agent I had a valid license, but wouldn't give the agent the driver's license number.

By now the agent had heard enough of the conversation that he decided I was honest (despite the cowboy hat and the funny accent), and I got the car and made it in time for the salad!

When you get your car, walk around it before you get in and drive off. I picked up a car one dark, rainy night in

Washington D.C., after a 3-hour late plane ride and before a 6-hour drive to the Southern tip of the DelMarVa peninsula. As I approached the exit I stepped out to take off my coat, and spotted a scratch that ran the full length of the passenger side, a broken taillight and a crunched rear fender. Think they would believe that I didn't do it after I came back from my trip? Not a chance! Always "check it out" before you "drive it out".

Another simple, but good idea is to try the most important switches to find out how to turn on lights, air conditioning, radio, and other accessories. I've had to pull off the road more than once in the dark trying to find out where the light switch was on some Japanese car whose name I couldn't pronounce. I've known people who've popped the hood up at 55 miles per hour trying to turn on the lights.

Also, it's a good idea to learn how to "pop" the gas cap cover. On one trip I rented a car in Dallas, drove to near Wichita Falls, drove back to Dallas late, late that night and attempted to fill up the car. I pushed and pulled everything that looked like a lever; even got out the owner's manual and climbed in the trunk (all in the rain) trying to get the gas cap cover off. I never did get it open. The car rental agency was kind enough to fill it with gas that cost $2.50 per gallon.

Finally, if you ever lock your keys in your car, don't break out the window. Call a locksmith. And if there's no other choice, break out a big side window — they cost less than those little vent windows.

CHAPTER XII

FOR FEE OR FOR FREE

– Turn your cold hard experiences into soft warm cash.

YOU COULD BECOME A PRO

"How much would you charge to come to speak to our annual meeting"? That simple yet shocking question marked the first time I began to think of myself as a professional speaker. Up until that time I had primarily given a few speeches as part of my job. I was a corporate economist for a large bank. Part of my job was to speak to a variety of groups across the country about economic forecasts. One of the reasons I got into humor was that so many people laughed at my predictions that it was a natural. I slipped over into deliberate humor rather than unexpected humor. Nevertheless, my point is that somewhere in your speaking career, that phrase will pop up, or it may pop up in your own head and you will begin the long journey of moving from a free or non-paid speaker to a fee-paid professional speaker.

If you are not intending to become a paid professional speaker, this chapter may not interest you. However, if you are someone who is very intent on being either a part-time or a full-time, paid, professional speaker; and if you are struggling with Who, What, When, How, How Much, and If to charge a fee, this chapter will help you.

WHEN DO YOU START ASKING FOR A FEE?

Zig Ziglar, the famous motivational and sales trainer, often makes the statement that he gave over 3,000 "free" speeches before he gave his first "paid" speech. The number of free speeches I gave was probably less than 300. In fact, I frankly never thought of becoming a professional speaker until a late night phone call in 1981. "What would you charge to come speak to my annual meeting?", said the voice on the line—and I was a professional speaker quite by accident.

I was lucky. I didn't have to decide "when" to start asking for a fee. When someone offers to pay you for your speaking services, you have passed from being a public service speaker and into the transition period of a potential professional speaker. (I use the word potential because certainly not everyone desires to take their abilities to that point.)

Maybe you're not as lucky in this area.   During this transition period between public service and professional, your greatest struggle is probably with your self-image. You may be having a difficult time getting up the confidence to actually ask for a fee when someone invites you to speak. Follow this rule: When you think you should have a fee for speaking, ask. You'll never get it if you don't ask for it.

Most speakers put off asking for a fee far too late into their careers, often get discouraged, and give it all up. If you're getting lots of invitations to speak, over one a month, I'd say you're ready.

HOW MUCH SHOULD YOU CHARGE?

Zig Ziglar once told an aspiring young speaker to ask what you think your worth. If the meeting planner doesn't have that amount of money ask them how much they do have, then do it for that amount of money. If they don't have any money, do it for free. This is sage advice for beginning speakers who need the combination of experience, confidence, and cash.

WHO DO YOU CHARGE A FEE?

I know several speakers who do a great number of "freebee" speeches—probono. Regardless of your fee, if you choose to do one at a significantly reduced rate, or for free, the last thing you want to do is diminish your perceived value. If you're a $10,000 a night speaker and you do freebees now and then, sooner or later someone is going to decide that you are not a $10,000 a night speaker. The same is true if you are a $500 speaker.

If you significantly reduce your fee or do one for free, always write the amount of the fee in your letter of agreement (your normal fee), mark through it, then write "gratis", "probono", "no fee", above it in handwriting. This helps establish your value and lets the meeting planner know that you are doing them a special service.

The first time I was asked "how much?", I asked for $100. (I had no idea that people actually made a living doing this at that time; in fact, I considered it a rare privilege to have an opportunity to speak.) The fee was not a problem. In fact, I later found out the meeting planner had a budget of $500 for the speaker.

If you are a speaker considering going full-time, I would hope that your fee is well established in a range from $500-$1,000, but if not, I'd keep your regular job until you get to that point. And it may not mean that you are not a $500-$1,000 speaker, but it may mean that your marketing effort is not sufficient to put you in contact with meeting planners with a budget at that level.

There's an old saying in this business that you can be successful one of two ways—you can be a good speaker, or you can be a good marketer. Some professionals in this industry are one or the other. The ultimate goal is to be very good at both.

WHEN TO INCREASE YOUR FEE

It is my firm belief that a good speaker should always be increasing his/her fee. Here's why. Three reasons.

First, the more you speak, the more experience you get, the better you get at delivering your material, the more you will believe yourself to be worth. This is what I call "self-image fee setting". As your self-image about your presentation and performance ability improves, the fee you will ask will also increase.

Secondly, your fee should be going up because of the services you offer. If you can develop a membership sales seminar for an association, a customer service seminar, a sales seminar, or a stress reduction seminar, in addition to a keynote or some other service you already offer, then you are adding value to what you do and that extra value should command a fee increase.

Thirdly, as your marketing skills become more refined, you will hopefully be working to find yourself in newer and better markets. As you find yourself in these newer and more sophisticated markets, your fee must be appropriate. Beware of this pitfall. I know some speakers who have moved their marketing efforts into new levels of markets, say from regional or local organizations to state and national organizations. Their fees did not increase. When this continued over a period of two or three years they found they had saturated a good part of the state and national markets at lower fee schedules and had no place to go to make the next move in fees without a very horrendous jump.

My point is you can be too cheap for a market. If you are marketing yourself to national associations and your fee is still $100, you're probably not going to get many jobs. The reason? National associations don't hire $100 speakers. They want a speaker in line with the budget they allocate for their annual meeting. I've lost many jobs over the years to speakers whose fees were 15 to 200 percent greater than mine, simply because their fee was more appropriate for the group. By the same token, I have booked speeches that speakers (and very good speakers) were denied because their fee was only half mine.

BUREAUS AND FEES

If you ever have the opportunity to work with a bureau, you will find that the first question they ask a meeting planner who calls is "What is your budget?". If the budget of the meeting planner is $2,000, for example, then the bureau sends out information about appropriate speakers who charge $2,000. Obviously, before a speaker charges $2,000 with a bureau, the bureau will have checked him out and will have found that he is in fact close to that in value.

I have found one of the great advantages of working with bureaus is their promotion at new fee levels helps establish you at those new levels. In other words, let's say I am contemplating a move from $500 to $750.

I inform the bureaus I work with so we're all quoting the new fee. If I start booking speeches at that level out of my office, and bureaus are also doing it, and doing it again and again, then it is obvious that fee level is appropriate.

In regard to bureaus, I highly recommend trying to stay consistent with the fee you quote in your office and in the bureau office. Countless times we have had meeting planners call our office directly and the bureau as well to check up on us to see if we were legitimate in our fee. It could be very embarrassing if you quoted a fee of 75% of what you were telling the bureau to quote. And it could cost you a lot of business.

CONTRACTS

Should you use a contract? That's strictly up to each individual; however, I have found that a simple letter of agreement outlining the terms of our discussion with the meeting planner suffices very well. Anyone who is going to be dishonest is not someone I could speak for with full enthusiasm anyway. Some speakers require a deposit with the initial booking. I do not. Occasionally, a meeting planner may cancel an engagement due to unforeseen circumstances. Obviously, if all or part of the fee was paid up front, the likelihood of a flippant cancellation is reduced. However, unforeseen events can arise causing the cancellation of entire meetings. Set your own policy. Some speakers have written in their letter of agreement a penalty for cancellation depending upon how close to the engagement date it occurred.

We prefer to not consider it a cancellation, but a postponement and work toward filling their needs when another date is set. Unfortunately, from time to time, there's no opportunity for rescheduling and it's a real cancellation.

Our policy is that when we have a cancellation, and it is a date which we passed up other engagements, we ask for a cancellation fee of 30 to 50 percent of the total fee. We don't always get it. Sometimes we get a fee that is less than the amount we ask for, but we've always gotten something in return for our holding that date, particularly, if flight arrangements have already been made and that stop is part of a "tour" of several speeches.

NEGOTIATION

At one time in my career, I set my fee at a certain level and only in extreme circumstances did I budge from that level. Early in your career the closer you can adhere to that philosophy, the better you will be. People will always be trying to talk you down to a lower fee and the greatest disadvantage is that if you consistently let yourself be talked into doing $500 speeches when you normally charge $1,000, sooner or later you'll begin to think like a $500 speaker instead of a $1,000 speaker. This mindset will carry over into your performance and could be hard to overcome.

Fee structure negotiation is always a matter of personal preference. Currently, we do negotiate if we can do multiple bookings with a client. For example, if I can do six in a row for one client, I will certainly do that at a lower fee per engagement than I would do one single engagement for only one client. By the same token, if I can get a solid guarantee of future and ongoing business, I will negotiate.

Because I have other business interests and a young family, if I can get to an engagement and return home in the same day or evening I will negotiate. However, in this latter case, I would never cut my fee more than 25 percent and even in the case of multiple bookings I would never advise cutting your fee more than 50 percent. I will also reduce my fee if the meeting planner has a special function where several meeting planners will be in attendance and the opportunity for future business exists.

Certainly, I know speakers who normally charge $1,500 but will go do a meeting for $200 because they have the philosophy that "some nights I sit at home and don't make $200". Again, that is a matter of personal preference. However, let me leave you with two observations. First, I have seen more problems arise in cases where I "bent" and lowered my fee, than in cases where I received my normal fee. In fact, I have actually seen speakers lose potential jobs because they agreed to cut their fee just to be considered for the engagement.

One way my office attempts to handle meeting planners with lower budgets is to recommend speakers in those price ranges, if we are comfortable with them. In fact, we have worked with three or four aspiring speakers over the years who have full-time jobs, who do not want to speak full-time, but are very interested in developing that aspect of their lives. They are very good speakers who we have begun to help with their marketing.

This concept has given us an opportunity to provide speakers to clients whose budget will not fit my fee schedule at the present time, and allows us to keep a good relationship with that customer, knowing that some day he may in fact have the budget for my fee. Many times meeting planners will be out of money one year and have more than enough for your fee the following year. Plus, helping some new speakers market themselves has been a great benefit to us, and to them as well.

THE MECHANICS OF GETTING PAID

Some speakers I know get paid everything up front when they book the engagement. Others get half up front and half after the presentation. A few wait until they return home and bill for the services.

The same is true of billing for travel expenses. Some estimate the travel expenses and get them up front. Others bill after the event.

I do like to be presented with a check (or the balance of my fee if we received an up-front deposit) immediately following my presentation for a couple of very good reasons.

First, it is like another round of applause or another reward for doing a good job. It is always nice to walk away with a warm feeling in your heart and cold cash in your pocket.

The second reason I like to pick up the check is that sometimes it can be as much as 30 to 60 days before you have your check if you wait to get home to bill for your fee. We've had a couple of instances where it took as long as 100 days in order to get paid. Unfortunately, this was a bureau booking and it took both my office and the bureau office to lean on the client and finally get their treasurer to write a check.

On one occasion I had a meeting planner come to me after the presentation and tell me that he did not have enough money in the treasury to pay my fee. He then asked if I would rather he pay me what he had or wait until he got all of it. I assure you I took what they had and six months later we finally retrieved the rest. Also, personnel change is inevitable and we have had one or more occasions where the person to whom the billing was sent left their position and their replacement did not know that the "account payable" existed.

If you do have to check up on your check, I would suggest always approaching it from the stand point that "We are going through our records and noticed that we have not received the check for the November presentation. We wanted to call to see if there was something else we needed to provide you." That will get the ball rolling. Always make it look as though it is your fault. I have yet to see a meeting planner who deliberately refuses to pay a speaker although I have heard that it happens.

CHAPTER XIII

PROMOTING YOUR SPEAKING

– Market your message and your mouth with your mind.

Without a doubt, the best, most cost-effective, promotion of your speaking talent is to give a good speech every time. But there are a few additional things you can do. Some of the following are free, some are priceless, some are costly. They all work.

LET THE WORLD KNOW WHAT YOU DO

I've met a lot of speakers with exceptional talent who acted as if they wanted to keep it a secret—then couldn't figure out why they never got asked to speak.

The number of groups that have meetings in this country is seemingly infinite. And they are all looking for speakers— both free and professional speakers. Plus, once you speak to one type of group you find they have sister organizations, and the audience members belong to other groups who need speakers. In fact, every person in every audience is a potential client.

Ever hear of the Law of 250? A car salesman in Detroit developed this theory in the Mid 70's after attending a couple of funerals. He noticed the funeral director always had just the right number of memorial cards for each service. The funeral director had noticed over the years the average attendance at a funeral was about 250. In other words, each person has about 250 people in his inner circle of relatives and close friends that care enough about him or her to attend their funeral. These are the same people you'd invite to your wedding or special celebration. Make a list of your 250, then let them know—again and again.

One speaker sent birth announcements to his list of 250 announcing the birth of his new avocation. Then as he developed his speeches he sent another announcing the birth of each one as follows:

Announcing the birth of a new fun-filled motivational speech.

Name: ...... *The Buffalo Ballet in Tu-Tu Time*
Time: .... *January 1, 1992*
Length: .... *30-45 minutes*
Weight:..... *Light-hearted*
Features: . *Motivational*

Another speaker let his 250 know through Christmas letters. Find your own way and have fun with it.

Introduce yourself to strangers and let them know what you do. Most will be fascinated and some will want to hire you. I have booked speeches with people I've met on airplanes, in hotel lobbies, and on hotel elevators. As you travel, remember that most people travelling are potential clients. As one speaker put it, "I love to work airplanes, 'cause once they close the door the prospects can't get up and leave."

SHOULD YOU HAVE A BROCHURE

I know some speakers who have developed fantastic careers without a brochure—but not very many! My advice about brochures is this—get one. If you are going to get paid to speak you had better leave the impression you are qualified. A brochure does two things. First, it demonstrates your ability to others. Second, it demonstrates your ability to yourself. I don't think I really ever saw myself as a professional until after I saw myself in my first brochure.

In fact, after developing my first brochure, I was much more impressed with my own ability to speak. It made me more confident I could succeed and compete. Plus, it psychologically backed me into a corner and forced me to go forward, because once I started getting brochures in circulation I was publicly committed — no turning back!

Don't worry about creating a masterpiece the first time. Not until I developed my fifth brochure design did I finally feel comfortable with my work. Each brochure was the best I knew how to do at that time. But as I learned more, each one got better and better until I got comfortable and moved on to other promotional materials.

Don't worry about spending a lot of money. A brochure can be 2 sides of a letter-sized card (8 1/2 X 3 1/3) or it can be four pages like a newsletter. It can be black and white or glorious four-color. Do what you're comfortable with. Get a couple of good pictures — one flattering shot and at least one of you speaking — and put them in.

Tantalize the reader with biographical information and achievements, but don't overdo it. Concentrate not on your "features", but on the positive "benefits" your speaking will have for the meeting planner and his or her audience.

Look at other speakers' brochures. I actively solicit the promotional materials of my peers in the business to see how my material stacks up. Don't be afraid to ask other speakers for their brochures. In fact, I like to get other speakers' entire promotional packets, to analyze and compare to my own.

Before you get too carried away with your brochure, let me

remind you it's not everything. It's only one part of your total package as a speaker. It should be complementary to your personality, your appearance, your speech, your style, your stationary, your promotional folders, and all your printed materials. It should fit in with all you are and do. And it should be appropriate for your niche.

Keep it simple. I've seen so many unbelievably elaborate brochures and related materials that I've chosen to keep my promotional pieces very simple. In fact, I believe mine stands out in its simplicity.

Use ink colors (permanent colors—ask your print shop), letter styling, and paper texture that show consistency from one printed piece to the next. Don't send out a four-color glossy brochure in a plain white envelope with a hand written return address. Look consistent, professional and successful!

BUSINESS CARDS

I hand out brochures instead of business cards. Most business cards rarely get looked at a second time. It's tougher to throw away a brochure, most will keep it!

Plus, I don't like to hand out business cards (or brochures in my case) with out getting one back. Why? Many times your card or brochure gets set aside, filed, or lost and you've lost a potential speaking engagement. Always ask for THEIR card. In fact, when someone approaches me about a card, I prefer to say "I've got one here somewhere but if you'll give me yours I'll send you one when I get back to the office".

I now have their address and telephone number. I can find out if they have a meeting date and when. I make notes on their card. My staff will then follow up with a brochure and a letter, let them know we'd like to work with them to make their meeting a success, and follow up again in 2 weeks with a phone call.

You'll get far more bookings out of the cards you "get" than the card you "give". If they don't have a card, hand them a piece of paper (I keep a yellow legal pad out for this very purpose). Ask them to write their name, address and telephone number, or do it yourself...so you can read the writing later.

Ask for business during a presentation. Some speakers make a point of mentioning during the latter part of their presentation "If you have a group in mind you'd like to have me speak to, please come up afterwards and visit with me." Lighten it up by following up with something funny like "I've got small kids and it's the only time I get to get a good night's sleep" or "I like to bring my spouse 'cause he (she) does all the driving and all I have to do is sit there and hold the wheel." A word of caution: Don't carry this too far. Some meeting planners may object to providing you with a forum for free advertising.

Promotion is a process, not a project. Always leave them something. Some professional speakers feel strongly that you should leave some informational piece in front of everyone in your audience — even a keynote audience. This could range all the way from a business card or a simple typewritten page with some of your gems on it, to an elaborate brochure, full packet, or book.

Some speakers have a favorite poem or summary of their points printed attractively and "suitable for framing" that they provide to everyone. Of course, it always includes their name, address, and telephone number.

This kind of promotional material can be pre-arranged on or above the dinner plate; handed out during your presentation; left at the back so each can pick one up as they leave; or "handed out" by helpers as they leave.

Give them an opportunity to take a part of you home...and they'll remember you when they need a speaker!

WHAT'S YOUR NICHE AND WHERE DO I ITCH?

I didn't realize it when I started speaking, but I had a niche market. Agricultural groups and associations. And those folks have lots of meetings. As time has passed that niche has expanded, but that's where I started and it's still a big part of my business.

Now, ask yourself: "What's my niche?" If the answer doesn't come quickly, then ask yourself: "What do I know most about?", "What types of people do I get along with best?", "What groups would I best fit?".

Once you determine the groups, find a mailing list. For associations, there's a huge directory that includes most in the United States. For agricultural groups, there's another directory available. For state associations there's another directory. Be a bird-dog and find every mailing list for your niche that you can find. In fact, each one you find will likely lead you to many more. Call me if I can help.

A past President of the National Speakers Association had a great saying that's always stuck with me about promotion and sales. He said, "Get 1,000 good prospects and mail them something every month." His point is this, mailing promotional pieces is not a one shot effort; it's not a project, it's a process.

Before you mail, though, do some qualifying. That is, why mail to someone who couldn't, wouldn't, can't or doesn't need to hire a speaker. How can you tell if they can or can't? — Call 'em up and ask 'em.

Why call? Because the call will be cheaper than the $3.00 worth of envelope, brochure, letters, and labor you're getting ready to put a stamp on and send.

What do you say when you call. Here's a suggested script:

FIRST CALL SCRIPT
Be Friendly! Help Them Do Their Job

I'd like to speak with whomever is in charge of meeting and convention planning for your organization please. (If in meeting - "Does that mean he/she can't be disturbed?" If they do connect me, say "_____, thanks for taking my call. I was told you were in a meeting. Would it be better if I call you back this afternoon or tomorrow?")

_____, my name is Laura Williams. I work with Dale Minnick, a professional humorist & motivational speaker from Oklahoma. I was given your name as the person in charge of meeting planning for _____. Is this correct?

I wonder if you could help me. I'm calling because Dale has worked with _____ and been very successful. I can't claim that he can do that for your organization, but I'd like to ask you a few quick questions, then I'll be able to tell you quickly Yes, we can help. Or No we can't. Then you can tell me how you'd like to proceed.

_____, what kinds of meetings do you have? When are they held? When do you begin planning for those/that meeting? What are your objectives for your next meeting?

What kinds of speakers have you used in the past? May I ask who? What kind of process do you use in selecting speakers? When will the final selection of speakers be made? What kind of budget for speakers do you generally have?

_____, from what we've discussed, Dale could be a tremendous addition to your program. Dale speaks all across the country, doing Humorous/Motivational Keynotes as well as very customized, very entertaining seminars on customer service, sales, and association membership development. His recent clients include the Texas Bowling Ball Assn., the Idaho and Pennsylvania Spitball Assn., Nat'l. Shuffle

Board Assn. etc. He is active with other business interests of his own, and so he has a great rapport with audiences like yours.

Would you like to receive further information about Dale? Is there any specific type of information you would like to have? (If ask about fees, don't quote over the phone. "Let me include a fee schedule in the packet" or "Let me include a package price in the packet")

One last quick question. Should you decide to hire Dale, you and who else would make the decision? What is their position? By the way, whose opinion would you want before finalizing that decision? (How many people are on the committee? Would you like to receive separate packets for your board/comm. members? We'd be glad to send the information directly to your committee, we've found that to be helpful to other groups in the past. IF YES GET ADDRESSES.)

Thank you very much for your time.

DOUBLE CHECK ADDRESS!

A great rule for promoting to potential clients is this: Never, Never, Never mail without following up with a call. And never, never, never call without following up with something you mail...even if it's just a thank-you note for taking time to visit with you on the phone.

Finally, never, never, never, give up contacting new prospects. I can't tell you the number of times one of my staff has had a prospect be rude or even hang up on them, then 6 months later call back to book a speech. Don't give up working to get UP IN FRONT.

CHAPTER XIV

BOOKING SPEAKING ENGAGEMENTS

– Work hard to make it easy for your meeting planner.

THE TELEPHONE

I have never booked a speech for someone who called my office or home—that is, unless the telephone got answered. Most speeches are booked by telephone. All the promotion in the world won't accomplish anything if you don't answer the meeting planner's call.

At the very least, if you can't be there, get an answering machine and put a cute message on it.

If you operate out of your house, get a second line put in, put that number on your brochure and letterhead, and always answer that number as a business. If you aren't home days, then try to find a pleasant, homebound person (consider a handicapped person who is good on the phone) and "call forward" to their number during "business hours".

Respond as quickly as possible. If the caller has a date in mind, let's say February 10, and you haven't got a speech booked for six months before or after that date, don't let on. Always be busy.

Here's an example of how to respond "February is a busy month, let me get the calendar and check on the 10th". If you've got another engagement that week, say "I'm doing the Bowling Green Bowling Ball Association (or whatever it is) in Minneapolis that week but, let's see, Yes! The 10th is open! May we put that date on hold for you?"

HOW MUCH ARE YOU?

Whether you're selling a car, a house, a bowling ball, or a speaking engagement, one of the first questions you usually hear is "How Much is it?"

Price is always a great concern, but really not as great in importance. Value, not price, is the key concern. My office staff works diligently to accurately represent my value and they always try to put the price off to the last.

We do have a set schedule of fees. However, before we can talk price with a meeting planner, we need to know what their needs are. My fee for a banquet speech is different than my fee for full-day seminar on Teamwork and Customer Service, complete with 200 workbook-style handouts.

Find out the needs of your meeting planner by asking open-ended questions like these:

1. Tell me about your meeting.

2. Do you have a date picked out?

3. How many people do you expect?

4. Do you use your banquet speaker for another portion of your program? (They may never have thought about doing that until you mention it.)

5. Who have you had in the past?

6. When do you anticipate making a final decision?

Here's why we ask these questions. First, if their meeting is a 3-day affair, there may be an opportunity for me to do a banquet speech, then stay over and do a seminar, creating higher income for me and saving travel expenses for another speaker for them.

Secondly, we need to know the date of their meeting. If I'm already booked on that date, there's no point getting too deep in negotiations. Instead we need to see if they have any flexibility in moving that date, or if not, let's focus on booking a subsequent meeting.

Thirdly, we need to know if the group consists of 20, 200, or 2,000. Generally the bigger the groups the bigger the budget.

Fourth, knowing who they've had in the past tells us how big a factor the "price" will be. After a short time in the speaking business, you will develop a feel for the ball park fees of a wide variety of speakers. Obviously, if they had Paul Harvey the year before, they either have a big budget, or they're totally out of money!

We always summarize the benefits of my speaking to their group before we announce the fee. "Dale would love to come and entertain and inspire your group like he's done for many others like your's this year. His professional fee is $7.32 plus travel expenses. Does that fit your budget?"

If it doesn't fit, they'll usually respond pretty quickly with exactly what their budget is. If we're close but not quite enough, we'll ask them about doing a seminar to save the expenses of another speaker, or we'll suggest ideas for private sponsorship, or we'll ask them if their travel budget will come out of a different account. If we still can't get together, we'll work to recommend another speaker who fits their budget.

DO YOU HAVE SOME INFORMATION YOU COULD SEND ME?

No Problem. Many meeting planners are representing a planning committee who will make the ulitmate decision. We'll assemble a packet of information that includes brochures (send enough for everyone on the committee so each one can get their own — they may belong to other groups — plus few other speakers ever do it), a biographical sketch, a list of recent and upcoming clients, a newsletter, 6-8 recommendation letters from similar groups I've spoken for, and a demo video or audio cassette if requested.

We don't send videos or audios unless requested. I prefer to encourage them to call my most recent clients in their industry and talk to them. Why? Because I work hard to get to know each audience and customize each speech to fit each group and the things going on around them. That's hard to pick up in a tape, but easy to communicate over the phone with another meeting planner. Plus, our relationships with meeting planners extend from long before to long after the actual speech.

We mail this information, along with a "promotional letter" all enclosed in an attractively designed folder, to the meeting planner. Some speakers like to draw out this mail presentation by mailing a letter one day, a folder with information 2 days later, and the video or audio another 2-3 days later. Their thought is that it heightens the anticipation of the meeting planner.

We also inform them that we've put their date on our calendar to "hold" it and that our policy is that we will not book over that date until they make a decision or until we have consulted them first. This has never been a problem. Usually when we get an inquiry on a date we're already holding, the first client feels "Somebody elses wants him, we better go ahead and firm this up".

The letter in the packet tells the meeting planner when we'll be following up to learn of their decision.

YES, WE WANT YOU!

Music to my ears. Once they confirm a solid booking, we send out a "confirmation packet". It includes only five items:

1. Two letters of agreement, signed by me, one for them to sign and send back.

2. Another biographical sketch.

3. A glossy photograph, more than one if they need it, for use in publicizing their events.

4. An information questionaire for them to complete and mail back. See appendix.

5. An introduction. (See Chapter 6)

Booking speeches requires good salesmanship, integrity, and prompt response to requests. Being up front with your meeting planner will get you UP IN FRONT again and again.

CHAPTER XV

THANK YOU, THANK YOU, THANK YOU

– Appreciation and professionalism go hand in hand.

The two most important words in the English Language are Thank You. And we look for every opportunity in my office to say Thank You to people we work with around the country.

SAYING THANK YOU TO PEOPLE I'VE MET

On my way home after a speech, I make a list of people I want to send Thank You letters. We start with a standardized letter for three groups of people, those I met, those I used in my program, and those wanting follow-up information. Then, I either write personal notes in long-hand if I need to, or we'll incorporate my personal note into the body of the letter. Plus, at the bottom of each letter is a postage stamp size picture of my smiling face staring up at them.

FOLLOW-UP WITH THE MEETING PLANNER

My speech may be over, but my relationship with the meeting planner is not.

As soon as possible after I return home, I summarize my

expenses and prepare a statement. The statement is mailed with a Thank You letter to the meeting planner.

Included in the Thank You letter is a polite request for a letter of recommendation and evaluation. Why do I want a letter back? Because this meeting planner's recommendation letter, added to all the others I receive, are the keys to more speaking engagements with similar clients.

For example, if I get an inquiry from the California Spitball Association and I'm able to send them a promotional packet with a letter from the Idaho Spitball Association that says I'm a great speaker, odds are I'll be going to California!

My experience is that 29 out of 30 clients will write that letter of recommendaiton. The other 1 out of 30 probably forget, but we don't pursue it further.

In addition to the Thank You letter, we send coffee mugs, cassette tapes, video tapes, and even flowers (to female meeting planners only). Plus, past meeting planners go on a newsletter mailing list and an opportunity list to receive information about new speeches, seminars, or books I've developed.

We also provide a more formal evaluation form to clients for whom I've presented seminars.

Occassionally, we review our marketing strategy and we'll contact the meeting planners to ask their advice or get their opinions about our marketing services. Then the Thank-You process starts all over again.

We also encourage past clients to call on us for recommendations for speakers for future meetings. We work to create a long-term relationship rather than a "wham, bam, Thank You man" approach. Plus, over time we see these meeting planners moving into positions of authority with other organizations and we want to be first in their mind.

THANK YOU TO YOU

Finally, I want to say Thank You to you for purchasing and reading this book. I hope that you found one idea, one inspiration, or one humorous story that will change your life. THANK YOU! Now go speak without fear and in a few years I'll be reading <u>your</u> book!

CHAPTER XVI

Humor For
The Time
Of Your Life

Now you're ready to spice up your speech with humor! If you haven't read Chapter II, go back and read it.

The 464 humorous entries in this chapter run the gamut from ad-libs to full-length stories. It is my intent they show you every style and type of humor.

Add them to your personal experience stories, adopt them as if your own, improve on them every way you can.

No other book has ever organized humorous stories to coincide with the times of your life. That will help you add your life to these entries. Turn the page and find lots of humor. Have the time of your life!

Humor For The Time Of Your Life

The Time Of Your Life:

Birth To Kindergarten

1. HEAVY FIREWORKS

I was a War Baby. My parents took one look at me and started fighting!

2. KIDDY KITTY

Four-year-old Tommy went with his dad to see a new litter of kittens. He returned breathlessly to tell his mother.

"There are three boy kittens and two girl kittens."

"How do you know that?", asked his mother.

Tommy replied, "Daddy picked each one up and looked...I think it's printed underneath."

3. BIG DOG

A youngster was presented with a huge German Shepherd for his birthday. He looked at the big dog in amazement, then turned to his father and asked, "Is he mine or am I his?"

4. SWIM AT YOUR OWN RISK

My 4-year-old daughter has a voice that'll carry from Dallas to Denver. During a break at a convention in San Antonio, all the attendees were lounging around the pool of the elegant hotel. "Daddy, Daddy," she screamed at the top her voice as she climbed out of the pool, "I just did something in the swimming pool I wasn't supposed to do."

Everybody heard her and they immediately climbed out with disgusted looks on their faces. Seeing the uproar she had created, she quickly ran over and in a whisper explained that the thing she wasn't supposed to do was...swim at the deep end.

5. SIMPLE SOLUTION

"Mommy, where are the matches?"

"Why?"

"We've got to build a fire under Jimmy. He swallowed the corn before we could pop it."

6. A TURN FOR THE WORSE

"Norman, why did you kick your little sister in the stomach?"

"Couldn't help it. She turned around too quick."

7. LEND A HAND

Six-year-old Nancy stood by the gate in front of her house looking into the street. In a while, a well-dressed man came by. "Hey, mister," she said, "would you mind opening this gate for me?"

"Glad to!" he said and pushed it. "Why couldn't you do it yourself?"

"Wet paint," she said.

8. CAN'T DO THAT

The six-year-old girl was raised on a farm and went to visit her grandmother in the city. Before she left home, the six-year-old was told by her mother that Granny was sort of old-fashioned about language. "Don't tell Granny that you have to go to the bathroom," said the mother. "Just tell her that you have to go powder your nose."

So the six-year-old came to visit Granny, and they had a great time. When at last it was time to leave, Granny told her: "You've been a nice little guest. And next time you come, you'll have to bring your little brother with you."
"Oh, I couldn't!" the little girl said. "He still powders his nose in his pants."

9. WHERE DID I COME FROM

My 5-year-old asked his mother where he came from, and after several attempts to satisfy his curiosity, she turned him to me. After several efforts to dodge the issue by telling him all about the flowers and bees, I finally told him everything...to which he replied he had just been kinda curious, 'cause the little boy next door said he came from Amarillo, Texas.

10. THE LAST SPANKING

The older lady in the Doctor's waiting room was getting annoyed at my over active 3-year-old daughter. Finally, she asked her sternly, "Have you ever been spanked?"

"Yes," said my daughter.

"And when did you have your last spanking?" asked the woman.

My daughter thought a minute and said: "I don't think I've had that one yet."

11. PLEASE REPEAT THE QUESTION

Trying to get all the kids involved the first day of kindergarten, the teacher asked the little boy, "Why do you sit in the corner scratching yourself?" He look up shyly and said, "'Cause I don't know where anybody else itches."

12. GOOD SWIMMER

Little Mark turned four and always had a lot of questions. One day after Sunday School, he crawled up in his Grandpa's lap and asked, "Grandpa, were you in the ark?"

His grandfather replied, "Why, No, son."

Mark looked at him strangely and said, "Then why weren't you drowned?"

13. HAVE A GOOD TRIP

The school nurse was showing slides on safety and first aid procedures to a group of second-graders. "Now what would you do if you saw one of your classmates trip and fall down a flight of stairs?" was the question. "I'd run to the office quickly for help," one little boy replied. "Good, now young man, what would you do if you saw a teacher trip and fall down the stairs?" He thought for a minute, then asked, "Which one?"

14. A GOOD LESSON

Jenny's mother ran into the bedroom when she heard her scream and found her two-year-old brother pulling her hair. She gently released the baby's grip and said to Jenny, "There, there. He didn't mean it. He doesn't know that hurts."

She was barely out of the room when the 2-year-old started screaming. Running back in, she asked, "What happened?"

"He knows now," replied Jenny.

15. WE MUST GO

My 4-year-old daughter and a 3-year-old neighborhood boy, walked hand in hand up to the front door of the house next door.

She had on a big Easter hat she'd 'borrowed' from her mother's closet, along with a pair of high heels 6 sizes too big. The boy borrowed an old shirt of mine (which drug the ground — the sleeves and the tail), an old baseball cap, and a pair of old cowboy boots he could have turned somersaults in.

Standing on her tiptoes, my daughter was just able to reach the doorbell. The lady of the house asked what she wanted and she said, "We're playing house and we decided to go visiting our neighbors. This is my husband and I am his wife. May we come in?"

Thoroughly enchanted, the lady said, "By all means, do come in."

Once inside, she offered the children milk and cookies, which they graciously accepted. When a second tall glass of milk was offered, my daughter refused by saying: "No thank you. We have to be going now. My husband just wet his pants!"

16. FROM SEA TO SHINING SNORE

My youngest son's name is Sage. He just started kindergarten and he's already having problems. When he was a baby I used to sing him to sleep with the Star Spangled Banner — personalized for him to sing: O, Sage can you see.... The problem he has now is every morning when they sing the National Anthem he goes to sleep!

17. A CHIP OFF THE OLD BLOCK

My 5-year-old looked up at me and said, "Dad, when I get big, will I be just like you?"

My chest swelled, I said, "Yes, my son."

He said, "I don't have to get big for a long time, do I?"

The Time Of Your Life:

1st, 2nd, & 3rd Grade Years

18. GENERATION GAP

A kindhearted old gentleman saw a little boy trying to reach a doorbell. The elderly man rang the bell and asked, "What now, little boy?"

"Run," said the boy, "that's what I'm gonna do."

19. ART TEACHER

"Do you know that Teacher has never seen a horse in her life?" exclaimed little Haley excitedly.

"What makes you think that?" asked Mother.

"Well," said Haley, "Teacher told us to draw something, and I drew a picture of a horse...and she didn't know what it was?"

20. MANNERS

FATHER: Well, Jackie, what did you learn at school today?

JACKIE (proudly): I learned to be polite and to say "Yes sir" and "No sir," and "Yes ma'am" and "No ma'am. "

FATHER: You did?

JACKIE: Yep!

21. COME CLEAN

"I sure wish you'd let me take my bath in the morning instead of at night," a first-grader said to his mother one evening. "Our teacher always asks us whether or not we've had a bath today, and I haven't been able to say yes all year."

22. NO RETURNS

The little boy's head bobbed up over the garden wall and a meek little voice called, "Please Mrs. Thompson, may I please have my arrow back?"

"Certainly," said the neighbor. "Where is it?"

"I think," the boy replied, "it's stuck in your cat."

23. EAR AND NOSE PROBLEMS

When my oldest son was 7, he got the flu and we took him to the doctor. The doctor asked him, "Have you ever had any trouble with your ears and nose?" "Sure," answered Greg, "they always get in my way when I take off my T-shirt."

24. HE WAS NORMAL

When his father returned from work, his son said, "Dad, there was a man here to see you this morning."

The father asked, "Did the man have a bill?"

The kid answered, "No, he had a nose like everybody else!"

25. PRAY FOR ME

My daughter Sarah was having dinner with my parents and they asked her to say grace. Everyone bowed their heads, but nothing came out.

"But what should I say?" she finally asked.

"Just say something you've heard your dad say," said my father.

She got a big smile on her face, she folded her hands under her nose, bowed her head and said, "My God, My God...where does all the money go?"

26. BE POLITE

Mikey and his mother were in the grocery store, and a clerk handed Mikey a candy bar.

"What do you say?" asked Mikey's mother.

Mikey screamed, "Charge it!"

27. DON'T TREAT ME THAT WAY

Small boy to his mother: "Don't yell at me; I'm not your husband."

28. LAST BITE

Mother: Do you like your new baby-sitter, Sheldon?

Sheldon: No, I hate her. I'd like to grab her and bite her neck like Daddy does."

The Time Of Your Life:

4th, 5th, & 6th Grade Years

29. SMART DOG

The man was talking to a 9 year-old boy about his talented dog. "I can't figure it out," he complained. "How is it that you can teach your dog all those tricks and I can't teach my dog anything at all?"

"Well," said the boy, "...for starters, you gotta know more than your dog."

30. SMART KID

My son is very perceptive. I told my him to go to the end of the line, but he came back and said, "Dad, there's someone already there."

31. WAIT

The safety sign read: "School Zone — Go Slow. Don't Kill a Child." Beneath it some kid had written: "Wait for a teacher."

32. HIGH AND DRY

My son, Greg, said to his teacher, "I'm going to be an astronaut when I grow up." "Do you really want to fly in space?" asked the teacher. "No," admitted Greg, "I just want to go eight days without takin' a bath."

33. WHAT IF

My wife told our 10-year-old daughter: "Don't play with boys. They're too rough."

My daughter Sarah thought a second and said: "What if I find a smooth one?"

34. I CAN DO IT

Our 9-year-old went to my wife when it began to snow and said,

"Can I put the snow chains on the car by myself? I know all the words."

35. PICK YOUR SPOT

Overheard at a teachers' meeting: "I prefer to teach in an elementary school. I know I'll have a place to park my car."

36. HARD TO LOSE

When he was 10 years old, his family almost lost him. His father wrote at the time...I should have taken him into the hills a little further.

The Time Of Your Life:

7th, 8th, & 9th Grade Years (Junior High)

37. READ 'EM AND WEEP

Paperboy: "There's a man on my route who has 34 different daily newspapers delivered to his place."

Friend: "Wow! He must be a well-read intellectual."

Paperboy: "Not really. He owns a pet shop."

38. DO'S and DON'TS

Mothers spend the first part of a child's life getting him to walk and talk, the second part, getting him to sit down and shut up.

39. GOOD EXAMPLE

Jimmie: "What is the difference in 'pro' and 'con'?"

Dad: " 'Pro' means the opposite of 'con'. These words may also be used as prefixes to other words. Do you understand what I mean?"

Jimmie, after thinking a moment: "Yeah, I think so. You mean like progress and Congress."

40. BRINGS HIS WORK HOME

A school teacher asked a little girl where her father worked.

"I don't know," replied the girl. "But I guess he makes rolls of toilet paper and light bulbs because that's what he brings home in his lunch box."

41. NICE CLOTHES

Eddie's problems started in the old days. There wasn't much money, all the kids had to wear hand-me-downs. It was a lot tougher on him than it was on his four older sisters.

42. AFFECTION

His mother loved him so much, she only hit him with the soft end of the mop.

43. SCHOOL FAVORITE

When he was a boy, he was the Teacher's pet. Teacher couldn't afford a dog.

The Time Of Your Life:

10th, 11th, & 12th Grade Years

(High School)

44. NERVES OF STEEL

An ironworker was nonchalantly walking the beams high above the street on a new skyscraper, while the pneumatic hammers made a nerve-jangling racket, and the compressor below shook the whole steel structure. When he came down, a man who had been watching him, stopped him. "I am amazed at your calmness up there. How did you happen to go to work on a job like this?"

"Well," said the other man, "I used to drive a school bus, but my nerves gave out."

45. DRIVE DAD CRAZY

My cousin was actually apprehensive about the guy his daughter was getting ready for. "I haven't met this guy your going out with," he said, "in fact, I don't know anything about him. Are you sure he's a good driver?"

"He sure is Dad. He absolutely has to be. If he gets arrested one more time, he loses his license."

46. HE DIDN'T LIKE ME

A teenaged girl tearfully told her girlfriend on the phone, "Yeah, I failed my driving test just because that examiner didn't like me. You could tell by the way he yelled at me when they were putting him in the ambulance."

47. GA GA GOO GOO I DO

Kids are getting married so young nowadays. Like the wedding I went to last week. The groom was so young his mother wouldn't let him have any wedding cake until after he finished his vegetables.

His parents were a bit unhappy about it but they attended the wedding. As their son repeated the vows and came to the part that says, "With all my worldly goods I thee endow...," the mother whispered to the father, "There goes the skate board!"

48. SHORT SHORTS

My Grandad never got used to girls wearing shorts in public. "Step-in's" he called them. One day he was sitting on his porch when a scantily clad young lady walked by. He turned to me and said, "Her laundry sure ain't gonna break no clothesline!"

49. GREAT NEWS

Teen-age son to father: "You'll be happy to know, Dad, I finally got my mind off girls. I've started thinking about women."

50. DISTINGUISHING FEATURE

It's still easy to tell the sexes apart, even though men are wearing long hair and women are wearing long pants. The one listening is the man.

51. YOU'RE ELECTED

When he graduated from High School, he was voted "Most Likely to Go to Seed".

52. FUN TRIP

Two Arkansas teenagers were eager to try the tunnel of love for the first time. "Shucks," the boy said later to a friend, "it was dark and we got soaking wet."

"How come?" his friend asked. "Did the boat leak?"

"There's a boat?"

53. A REAL GEM

Young man in jewelry store: "Please engrave this engagement ring, 'From Tim to Cindy.'"

Jeweler: "Take some advice, son, and just put, 'From Tim.'"

The Time Of Your Life:

College

54. NO PROBLEM

I have been reading about this college professor who has made his automobile run on fuel extracted from chicken manure. I'll bet he sure doesn't have any trouble with kids trying to siphon his gas!

55. SHUTTER SHUDDER

My Roommate in college was so dumb he thought a Polaroid was a condition you got from sitting on the ice.

56. IT'S A DUMP IN HERE

My year as a university faculty member was a lot like being a mushroom...they kept me in the dark, they piled on a lot of manure, and then I got canned!

57. A CLASSY DEFINITION

University: An institution that has room for 6,000 in its classrooms and 60,000 in its stadium.

58. GIVE HIM AN "A"

The chemistry teacher was giving his class a verbal quiz. "What," asked the college professor, "is the most outstanding result of the use of chemistry in the past five hundred years?"

"Blondes!" came the quick reply.

59. DON'T SEND ME BACK

Coed: "With this hectic college life, don't you wish you were a barefoot boy again?"

Student: "Not me, I was raised on a chicken farm."

60. NO MORE LICKS

A college boy said to his roommate, "The drought back home is really bad this time." "How can you tell?" asked his roommate. "I got a letter from Dad," he said, "and the stamp was fastened on with a paper clip."

61. KICK OFF!

University of Oklahoma graduate to University of Nebraska graduate: I understand ya'll had a big fancy wedding up at Lincoln the other day.

NU Grad: What do you mean?

OU Grad: I heard the bride's veil went all the way down to the cuff...on her overalls.

NU Grad: Well, one thing about our football players — we don't give 'em a letter — till they can tell which one it is. Besides, I figured out why you guys in Oklahoma use artificial turf instead of real grass on your football fields.

OU Grad: Why's that?

NU Grad: To keep your cheerleaders from grazing during halftime.

62. WATCH THE GOLD

I have a friend who, after finding out about the cost of college, just gave his son the money and let him retire.

63. NAME CHANGE

Bill: "I wish you boys wouldn't call me Big Bill."

Phil: "Why not?"

Bill: "These college names stick...and I'm going to be a doctor."

The Time Of Your Life:

Dating

64. THE GOOD OLD DAYS

Joe: "Whatever became of those old-fashioned girls who fainted when a boy kissed them?"

Laurie: "Whatever became of those old-fashioned boys who made them faint?"

65. BLUE LIGHT SPECIAL

One housewife to another, "My husband was working in a discount store when I met him. I should've realized then that he was a little off."

66. GIVE ME THE HAND

My father-in-law has a strange sense of humor. My wife and I had been dating for several months when I first met him. I thought I'd be proper and ask him for her hand so I asked, "Sir, could I have your daughter for my wife?"

He said, "Well, I don't know, trot your wife around here and let me get a look at her.

67. PEOPLE PREVENTERS

Dad: "Do you know what the best birth control method in the world is?"

Daughter: "No."

Dad: "That's it."

68. SPLINTERED LOVE

Jack: *"Are you still engaged to that girl with the wooden leg?"*

Jim: *"No. I got mad at her and broke it off."*

69. SHE'S BEEN CPR'D

Young man: *"Sir, I pulled your daughter out of the water and resuscitated her."*

Girl's Father: *"Then, by George, you'll marry her!"*

70. FOUND OUT

Jack: *"I just met a girl with a glass eye."*

Jim: *"How do you know? Did she tell you?"*

Jack: *"No, it just came out in the conversation."*

71. BLEEDING HEARTS

John is such a romantic guy. On their first date he took Judy out for coffee and cookies..., she just hadn't planned on giving blood that day.

72. SPEAK UP

I really like slow talking girls with Southern drawls! By the time they get done saying NO, they've already been kissed!

73. ADVICE FROM MY GRANDAD:

Beware, son, when you meet that girl with those bright enchanting eyes, that it's not just the sun shining through the back of her head.

74. ON HIS TOES

Uncle Wilbur's philosophy: *"It's better to love a short girl than never to have loved a tall!"*

75. CALL IN THE LIONS

According to my Grandad, love is a three ring circus: engagement ring, wedding ring, and suffering.

76. LOWER DOWN

Janet: *"I've got a soft spot in my heart for you."*

Joe: *"Let's get married."*

Janet: *"I said in my heart...not my head."*

77. TOO MUCH HELP

"Last week I ran an ad in the newspaper for a husband," said the spinster, *" and I got lots of replies. They all said, YOU CAN HAVE MINE."*

78. SINGULARLY HAPPY

"Why haven't you ever married?" the party hostess asked the eligible bachelor. *"Well, I'll tell you,"* he replied. *"I'd rather go through life wanting something I didn't have than having something I didn't want."*

79. ADVICE TO BACHELORS

Marry a girl from Moscow. She'll be happy, lovable, and used to following orders. Besides, your mother-in-law will live in Russia.

80. THAT'S ENOUGH

Jay: I have half a mind to get married.

Bob: That's all you need.

81. YOU BET

A man had been going with his girl for several years. Not once had he proposed marriage. His reason: he wanted to have a home, a car, and money in the bank before asking her. Finally one day he telephones her, saying "Dearest, I've got a home now, a brand new automobile and ten thousand dollars in the bank. Will you marry me?"

"I sure will, Honey," the girl replied. *"Who is this calling?"*

82. NOT TONIGHT

I should have guessed my wife was going to be a challenge to live with. After our first date, I walked her to her door, and asked her for a good, old-fashioned kiss. She went in and sent her grandma out!

83. NICE WHEELS

The more I learn about women, the more I love my pickup.

84. LIVE WIRE

One girl to another: There's never a dull moment when you're out with Wilbur...it lasts the whole evening.

85. AROMANTIC

Anyone who thinks chemical warfare is something new doesn't know much about women's perfume.

86. FORETHOUGHT

A boy and girl were out driving one evening. They came to a quiet spot on a country lane, and the car stopped. "Out of gas," said the boy.

The girl opened her purse and pulled out a bottle.

"Wow!" said the boy. "A bottle...what is it?"

"Gasoline," said the girl.

The Time Of Your Life:

Marriage

87. QUALIFIED FOR THE JOB

My aunt is a practical nurse...she married a wealthy, very sick, old man.

88. WE'RE RELATED

Buck had been drinking much too often, so Mrs. Ketchum suggested that Ethel rent a devil's suit and try to scare him into sobriety. Ethel thought that was a fine idea, and rented a Devil's suit at the costume shop. The next time Buck came home drunk, there was the Devil waiting for him at the door.

"Who are YOU?' exclaimed Buck.

"I AM THE DEVIL," said Ethel in a disguised voice.

"Well," said Buck, "Shake hands, brother, 'cause I married your sister."

89. PLEASE DON'T

Buck got stopped by a policeman and the policeman says. "You're going to get a ticket for speeding." Buck said, "Well I was only doing 40 miles an hour," and the policeman says, "No, you were doing 50 miles in a 30-mile zone." Buck said, "No, I was only doing 40." And then his wife, Ethel, popped up and said, "Don't argue with my husband when he's been drinking."

90. NONE WORSE

The policeman was questioning a drunk pinned under his own wrecked car, "Are you married?" "No, officer," replied the drunk. "Sho help me, this is the worsht fix I've ever been in my whole life!"

91. WHAT A MEMORY

Two men were discussing their wives. One said he loved his wife very much, but everytime they got into an argument, she became historical.

"You must mean 'hysterical'."

"No, 'historical'...she keeps bringing up the past."

92. CAN'T WATCH

Uncle Buck says he wears real dark glasses around the house because it bothers him to see his wife work so hard.

93. SIMPLE SOLUTION

Elmer is such a helpful husband. Ruby told him she would like to have a fur coat. Elmer suggested that she just quit shaving her legs.

94. RUN RUN

Uncle Buck claims he runs things around the house....the vacuum cleaner,...the washer,...the errands,...

95. SMART GAL

The wife who dresses to please her husband wears last year's clothes.

96. YOU DID IT

Every man needs a wife because many things go wrong that he can't blame on the government.

97. TAKE THE MONEY AND RUN

Do you have any trouble getting money out of your husband?"

"Not at all. I say I'm going back home to mother, and he immediately hands me the fare."

98. NO DEAL

Mary Jane: "The new mall's having a big sale...everything's really cheap."

Mary Jo: "I know. I told my husband about it. But then I discovered something even cheaper."

Mary Jane: "Really? What?"

Mary Jo: "My husband."

99. SHE'S SNEAKY

Mrs. Kelley: "Honey, I was talking to the painter. He said he could paint our kitchen for $300."

Mr. Kelley: "That's ridiculous. I could paint it for nothing."

Mrs. Kelley: "That's what I hoped you'd say."

100. SO'S HE

Aunt Violet: "Honey, would you please take the garbage out?"

Uncle John: "Just a minute...I'm waiting for something."

Aunt Violet: "Then I'll just have to take it out myself."

Uncle John: "That's what I was waiting for."

101. FALSE ALARM

My neighbor's wife dreamed she was in the arms of another man. Then she dreamed she saw her husband coming and yelled: "My husband!" My neighbor woke up and jumped out the window. He'll be out of the hospital in a couple of weeks. So will his best friend.

102. WALK A SPELL

Buck and Ethel had been married for 60 years. They made a good pair. He was knock kneed and she was bow legged. When they walked together, they spelled "OX".

103. THE GOOD OLD DAYS

Uncle Buck says: "I never knew what happiness was until I got married. By then, it was too late."

104. THE REAL PROBLEM

Marriage is a wonderful thing. It's the living together afterwards that causes all of the difficulties.

105. STOP THIEF

My wife says she stole all the towels out of the hotel room on our honeymoon because she didn't want it to be a total loss.

106. PRESCRIPTION FOR A HAPPY WIFE

After several months of married life, the glamour wore off and the young couple went to see a marriage counselor. After talking with the couple for a while and analyzing the problem, the counselor suddenly swept the woman into his arms and kissed her passionately.

"Now," said the marriage counselor. "This is the treatment your wife needs...Monday, Thursday, and Saturday, at least."

"Okay," replied the husband. "I can bring her in here on Thursday and Saturday nights, but Monday is my bowling night."

107. I WONDER

If a bride always wears white as a symbol of purity, why does the groom usually wear black?

108. RARE PAIR

If it weren't for my husband," she complained, "we'd be one of the nicest couples in town."

109. HELLO, HELLO

Marriage is like a midnight phone call—you get a ring, and then you wake up.

110. HAPPILY MARRIED

Some people ask the secret of our long marriage. We take time to go to a restaurant two times a week: a candlelight dinner, soft music, and a slow walk home. She goes Tuesdays; I go Fridays.

111. A GOOD SPORT

One of the wildest girls I ever met got married last week. I'm not going to say she fooled around but her bridal gown was plaid and the wedding announcement was on the sports page.

112. LOVE IS BLIND

The bride said, "Are you going to love me when I'm old and gray?"

The groom replied, "Why not, I've loved you through all the other colors. And not only am I going to love you...I'm going to write to you every day."

113. THANKS FOR THE WARNING

"Your wife has fallen into the well."

"Oh, that's all right. We use city water now."

The Time Of Your Life:

Work Life

114. WORKING

Not only is the horse just about extinct, so are the people who work like one.

115. MAKIN' FRIENDS

Abraham Lincoln was once taken to task by an associate for his attitude towards his enemies.

Why," he was asked, "do you try to make friends with them? You should try to destroy them."

To which Lincoln replied: "Am I not destroying my enemies when I make them my friends?"

116. EDUCATED FOOL

In the corporate offices there was a rule that only college graduates could be promoted above a certain level. The last three college men to assume responsible jobs with the administration bungled their jobs badly. Their departments were a mess and the company was in financial trouble.

This sign finally appeared just over the toilet-paper dispenser in the men's room: UNIVERSITY DIPLOMAS-TAKE ONE.

117. THOUGHTFUL DEFINITIONS

Business: What, when you haven't got any, you go out of.

Night watchman: A man who earns his living without doing a day's work.

118. NOT WORKING

My neighbor is so lazy that he married a pregnant woman.

119. YOU, TOO?

Worried office worker to boss: "Boss, sometimes I feel inadequate."

Boss: "Henderson, deep down inside everyone feels that way."

Office worker: "That they're inadequate?"

Boss: "No, that you are."

120. A BUREAUCRATIC SUCCESS

One man asked another: "What's your brother doing?"

"Nothing."

"But I thought he was trying to get a government job."

"He got it."

121. POUR THE CONCRETE

I don't know why everyone is saying the construction industry is in trouble. They just added two new wings to the unemployment building in my town.

122. ECONOMISTS, PHONE HOME

--Economists are often wrong, but never in doubt.
--Recent polls indicate that the public's respect for forecasters was only slightly ahead of stockbrokers and astrologers and well behind plumbers and sportscasters.
--Actually, though, economists often do agree; In those cases, however, they are always wrong.
--Harry Truman complained that economists are always saying, "...on the one hand this could happen, and on the other hand that could happen". Truman thought we needed more one-armed economists.
--Economists are like grasshoppers...they're great on distance, but they're not much on direction!

123. TOUGH LIFE

A farmer friend says he's used to hard times. "I got nothin' from my old man. Once on my birthday, he gave me a bat. The first day I played with it, it flew away."

124. HARD TIMES

Customer: *"How's business?"*

Owner: *"Terrible. Even the people who never pay have stopped buying."*

125. THANKS AND SO LONG

My poor cousin. In order to get the job they made him shave off his mustache, sideburns, and beard. And when they saw his face, they wouldn't hire him.

126. SURPRISE

My boss is such a romantic. Last Valentine's Day he surprised his wife with a slinky, black negligee? She was pretty shocked...never seen him in anything but boxer shorts.

127. GOOD, BAD, AND UGLY

Somedays he's a bad salesman...couldn't talk a customer out of a burning building.

Somedays he's good...he could talk a hungry dog off a meat wagon.

Somedays he's so ugly...bugs won't even hit the windshield on his side of the car.

128. I'LL RAISE YOU

Boss: *"Johnson, I've decided to start paying you on a commission basis...you'll get 10 percent of whatever you sell."*

Johnson: *"But I'm the office manager...I don't sell anything."*

Boss: *"In that case, make it 25 percent."*

129. SUE ME, SUE

The personnel director of a large concern told a newspaper reporter why his company does not hire women:

"Men do not want to work with the ugly ones and cannot work with the pretty ones."

130. NOT LONG

The counselor asked the employee how long he had been working at the company. He said, "Ever since they tried to fire me."

131. NEVER AGAIN

Tom and Joe worked on a construction crew. One day Tom noticed that the foreman always left the project about an hour early. "Say Joe," suggested Tom. "Why don't WE take off a little early too...just like the foreman." So they agreed to try it. As soon as Joe got home, he looked all over for Lena. Finally he opened the back door...and there she was sitting on the porch swing holding hands with the foreman. Joe silently closed the door and tiptoed out of the house. The next day he confronted Tom. "We better not try another stunt like we did yesterday. I almost got caught."

132. TRIBUTE TO MY BOSS

My Boss reminds me of a kerosene lamp. Not that he's steady and reliable. Actually, he's not especially bright; he smokes a lot; he gets turned down a lot; he's been burned out a few times; and he runs out of fuel just when you need him.

133. ON THE PAYROLL

My new ranch employee is quite a guy! He does the work of 2 men...Laurel and Hardy! In fact, having him around is like losing two good men.

134. WHAT A BOSS

His wife says he's good for his employees. 'Cause at night he talks in his sleep and says things like, "I'll raise you Fifty!"

135. I'VE HAD IT

Joe: "I feel like telling my boss off again."

Jack: "Again?"

Joe: "Yeah, I felt like telling him off last week, too."

136. SOUND DEFINITIONS

Consultant...knows a hundred ways to kiss, but never been out with a girl.

137. OOOPS

My cousin was fired because he couldn't leave his work at the office. He was a bank teller.

138. LAST CHANCE

Bank president: "Where's the cashier?"

Assistant: "Gone to the races."

President: "During working hours?"

Assistant: "Yes, sir. It was his last chance to make the books balance."

139. CLOSE IMITATION

Tom: "Why did Bill fire you?"

Ron: "Well, you know Bill's the foreman and the foreman is the guy who stands around and watches the others work."

Tom: "Yes, anybody knows that. But why did he fire you?"

Ron: "He was jealous. A lot of fellows thought I was the foreman."

140. GOOD QUESTION

Applicant: Before I take this job, tell me: Are the hours long?

Employer: No, only 60 minutes each.

141. EXHALE, INHALE

My secretary wears her clothes so tight that I can hardly breathe.

142. BAD BROKE

Taxpayer: "I'm so broke after paying my income tax that I'm being supported by an orphan in Vietnam."

143. COMPANY MAN

"Boss, I have to have a raise," the man said to his boss. "There are three other companies after me."

"Is that so?" asked the manager. "What other companies are after you?"

"The electric company, the telephone company, and the gas company."

The Time Of Your Life:

Husbands
And Wives

144. AIM TO PLEASE

"Won't your wife hit the ceiling when you come home?"

"Hope so. Last time she put a bullet through my hat."

145. MARITAL BLISS

"I shore wish I had my wife back," sighed the man from the Ozarks.

"Where is she?" asked a friend.

"Sold her for a jug of mountain dew."

"I reckon you're beginning to miss her."

"Nope, I'm thirsty again."

146. NO HELP AROUND THE HOUSE

"When I die, I want to be cremated," the man said.

"That would be just like you," replied his wife, "to go away and leave ashes lying all over the house."

147. NO DEAL

I wanted to get something for you, Dear, but no one would start the bidding.

148. HE AIN'T HERE

The main difference between a widow and a wife is that a widow knows where her husband is.

149. A WHITE LIE

Brown had occasion to reprimand his wife. "I think dear," he said soothingly, "that you fib a little occasionally."

"Well," she replied pointedly, "I think it's a wife's duty to speak well of her husband occasionally."

150. SURPRISE

What about the new bride who went through six boxes of cake mix trying to concoct a birthday cake for her husband? Every time she put the cake in the oven, the candles would melt.

151. FINANCIAL PROBLEMS

My wife can't ever balance our checkbook. We're so overdrawn, the bank called and wants their calendar back.

152. NICE DRESS

Did you hear the story about the lady who spent too much money on her dress? When her husband heard the price of the dress, he threw up his hands in anger and said, "How could you do it?"

The wife answered, "The devil made me do it."

He continued, "Why didn't you do like they do in the Bible and say 'Get thee behind me, Satan'?"

"I did," she answered, "and then I heard him say, 'It looks beautiful from behind, dear'!"

153. THANKS FOR THE COMPLIMENT

"Sam, a burglar in the kitchen is eating the stew I made."

"Go back to bed. I'll bury him in the morning."

154. GIVE HER CREDIT

I don't wish to imply my wife doesn't have a head for business, but when I told her we were overdrawn at the bank, she said, "No problem. I'll write a check to cover it."

155. CREDIT CARD KARATE

Tom: "Boy, your wife sure spends a lot on clothes."

Ron: "Yeah, she has a black belt in shopping."

156. DROP HER

My neighbor's wife had to let the maid go...because he wouldn't.

157. COLOR-BLIND

They say brunettes have a sweeter disposition than blondes and redheads. Don't believe it! My wife has been all three, and I couldn't see any difference.

158. READY, SET, GO

She is a light eater — as soon as it gets light, she starts eating.

159. ONLY TWO

My wife says I have only two faults — everything I say and everything I do.

160. BOOM!

No matter what she does with it, her hair looks like an explosion in a steel wool factory.

161. LOOK OUT DARWIN

Scientists say that man evolved from the monkey over several million years...but I've seen a woman make a monkey out of a man in a couple of seconds.

162. ODE TO LOCKS

"Women's hair, beautiful hair,
What words of praise I utter,
But, oh, how sick it makes me feel
To find it in the butter."

163. GREASE MONKEYS

Woman to attendant who had just brought her car from the garage: "What do you boys wipe your hands on when you run out of steering wheels?"

164. SAFETY FIRST

My friend bought life insurance and improved his wife's housekeeping at the same time—now she's even waxing the tub.

165. FROM RUSSIA, WITH LOVE

A man seeking a minor bureaucratic post in Moscow was asked to fill out a questionnaire. After he did, an official asked him what he meant in his reply to this question: "What is your attitude toward the Soviet Union?" The applicant replied, "As I wrote in the space, I feel deeply about the Soviet Union. It's like the way I feel about my own wife." "What do you mean?" said the official. "Well," the little man replied, "I wouldn't say like my own mother - but I do believe my attitude is the same as that toward my own wife."

Afterward, when he got the job, friends chided the meek clerk for ingratiating himself that way with the officials. He explained, "But I really do feel toward Russia the way I feel toward my wife. I don't love it, I can't change it, and I can't help dreaming of something better."

166. NOBODY CARES

"My wife doesn't understand me," he complained. Turning to his closest friend, again he cried, "My wife doesn't understand me! Does yours?"

"I don't know," his friend replied, "she never mentions you."

167. NIGHTY-NITE

Doctor: "Your husband must have peace and quiet and rest. Here are some sleeping pills."

Patient's wife: "But when should I give them to him?"

Doctor: "You don't understand—they are for you."

168. LET'S MAKE A DEAL

Harry: "I got some new golf clubs for my wife."

Dave: "Wow, that is great! I wish I could make a trade like that."

169. WHERE YA GOIN'

The average man's life consists of 20 years of having his mother ask him where he is going; 40 years of having his wife ask the same question; and at the end, the folks at the funeral wonder, too.

170. PRETTY WOMAN

Bragged the husband, "My wife is just as beautiful today as she was the day I married her." He paused and added, "Of course, it does take her longer."

The Time Of Your Life:

Having And Raising Children

171. GREAT VOICE

"Ethel," asked the choir director, "where did you get such a marvelous voice?"

"You have to be a good singer at our house."

"Why's that?"

"My husband and I have 8 kids and there's no lock on the bathroom door."

172. MY WIFE AND I

My wife and I were discussing the upcoming birth of our second child. "We'll have to move to a bigger house," I said. Our first-born listened gravely, then shook his head. "That wouldn't work," he said, "He'd follow us!"

173. THAT'S A GOOD QUESTION!

How many of you have sons?...Thank you. How many of you have daughters?...Thank you. How many of you have children...who are not sons or daughters?

174. GREAT TIMING

If anything makes my kids thirstier than going to bed, it's knowing that their mother and I have gone to bed, too.

175. BAD NEWS

For weeks the six-year-old kept telling his first-grade teacher about the baby brother or sister that was expected at his house. One day the mother allowed the boy to feel the unborn child kicking. The six-year-old was obviously impressed, but made no comment. Furthermore, he stopped telling his teacher about the impending event.

During show and tell one day, Tommy was at the front of the class and the teacher asked, "Tommy, whatever has become of that baby brother or sister you were expecting at home?"

Tommy burst into tears, hung his head, and confessed, "I think Mommy ate it!"

176. LET'S MAKE A DEAL

On the first day of school, each kindergartner arrived home with a note from the teacher, it read: "Dear Parents: If you promise not to believe all your child says happens at school, I'll promise not to believe all he says happens at home."

177. NO PROBLEMS

"Well, darling," said the little boy's mother as he walked into the kitchen, "were you a good boy at school today?"

"Sure," answered the lad. "How much trouble can you get into standing in a corner all day?"

178. WHAT'LL HE BE

"I hear you have a boy in college. Is he going to become a doctor, and engineer, or a lawyer, perhaps?"

The thoughtful answer was: "That I do not know. Right now the really big question is: Will he become a sophomore?"

179. AHH SO

The bride told her husband she wanted to stop at two children. When he asked her why, she said that she had read that every third child born in the world was Chinese.

180. SPRING CROP

A prominent farmer went in for his annual visit with his tax consultant and told him he wanted to use his son as a deduction.

"When was your son born?" the consultant asked.

"In January," answered the farmer, "but he was last year's business!"

181. UNDER WARRANTY

After having their fifth child, a couple received a playpen from their friends. Several weeks later the friend who sent the gift received this note of thanks: "The playpen is wonderful. Just what we needed. I sit in it every afternoon and read—and the kids can't get close to me!"

182. YOUR MISTAKE

"You sure ask a lot of questions," the father declared. "I'd like to know what would have happened if I'd asked as many questions when I was a boy. His son answered: "Maybe you'd be able to answer some of mine."

183. INVISIBLE NET

Son: How do they catch lunatics, Dad?

Dad: With lipstick, beautiful dresses, and pretty smiles.

The Time Of Your Life:

Hobbies & Sports I've Enjoyed

184. SEE THE STARS

I believe in astrology. I also believe you can see the future from a deck of playing cards. Yes, once I discovered six aces in a deck of cards— and immediately I knew the dealer was going to the hospital.

185. REARIN' TO GO

The Paul Revere cocktail: "Drink one and you start horsing around and waking up all the neighbors."

186. NOT THE WORST

Last year I had a speech out at Palm Springs and worked in 18 holes on one of their beautiful courses. I was doing pretty good for me and humbly said to the caddy, "I bet there are people worse at golf than I am." The caddy replied, "Probably, but they don't play."

187. YOU'RE CHEATING

Arnold: Howard's a cheat and I'm not playing golf with him again."

Jack: "How's that?"

Arnold: "Well, how could he find his lost ball a yard from the green when it was in my pocket?"

188. TEED OFF

Golf is a lot like taxes — you drive hard to get to the green and then wind up in the hole.

189. IDENTITY PROBLEM

My wife persuaded me to take her deer hunting. I found a good stand for her, told her not to move and left her alone. Soon I heard the sound of gunshots and raced back, fearing that she had shot herself. When I reached the scene, she was holding her gun on a man and shouting, "You leave that deer alone! I shot it, and it's mine!"

Replied the man shakingly, "If you say so, lady, it's a deer and it's yours, but just let me get my saddle off of it!"

190. NO HUNTING

The hunter from the city crawled through a posted fence with a loaded gun. He is survived by one widow, three children, and a rabbit.

191. SWEET FINISH

The steward at a race track caught an owner giving a drug capsule to his horse and said, "Hey, you can't do that — I'll have to report and suspend you." The owner said, "It's only a sugar cube." "Here, I'll eat one and here's one for you too." Later he told his jockey, "Just hold him back 'til the 3/4 pole — then let him go — if anything passes you, it will be either me or the steward."

192. THE LADIES' TEED

"Cecil," cried LaVonn, as he headed for the door, "You don't love me anymore! All you think about is golf. I bet you don't even remember the date we were married."

Cecil said, "Of course I do. That was the day I sank that 40-foot putt!"

193. HARD WATER FISHING

Two Texas ranchers were tired of the year-round heat and they decided to go to Canada in the winter to do some ice fishing. The trip took all day and all night.

As the sun came up they passed through a little Canadian village on the way to their fishing spot, stopped at the only store in town, and bought food, beer, and two ice picks.

Two hours later, one of them was back at the store to buy two more ice picks. Another hour later, he was back, "I think we're gonna need all the ice picks you got!" and bought every last one the storekeeper could find.

Curiosity getting the best of him, the storekeeper asked, "How's the fishing going?"

"Couldn't tell you," said the rancher, "we ain't even got the boat in the water yet!"

The Time Of Your Life:

My Church Life

194. THE POWER TITLE

A carnival had come to town and the strong man was challenging the villagers in this Southern community. "I will squeeze this lemon," declared the strong man, "and anyone who can squeeze ONE drop more from it after I am done...will be given one thousand dollars."

Several people tried it...but failed. Finally, a little, bald-headed, shriveled-up guy stepped forward and said he'd like to try. The strong man squeezed a lemon with all his might, reducing it almost to pulp. Then he handed the remains to the little wimpy-looking man...who then squeezed and squeezed and squeezed...finally extracting ONE drop of lemon juice.

The strong man was amazed. While he handed him the thousand dollars he revealed that this was the first time he had to forfeit the money. "Tell me, sir," said the strong man, "what do you do for a living?" In a quivering voice, the little guy confessed, "I'm the treasurer at the Baptist church."

195. BE SEATED

Wilbur and Zella had both retired. They had never been camping and they heard about a nice camp near Jackson Hole, Wyoming. Zella was worried about the toilet facilities, but she didn't want to use the word "toilet", so she wrote a letter to the campground owner. Around Minot, North Dakota where they lived, they used to call it an L.C., or Lavatory Commode. But she was so prim that she didn't want to say toilet or Lavatory Commode, so she simply asked in her letter if the camp had an L.C.

The camp ground owner read Zella's letter and was puzzled about the initials L.C. He finally decided it meant LUTHERAN CHURCH. So he wrote Zella the following letter:

"I am happy to inform you there is a local L.C. located only nine miles south of the camp ground. I realize this is kind of far if you are used to going regular. But, it's really a nice one...it seats 250 people. The last time my wife and I went was 6 years ago and it was so crowded we had to wait 20 minutes to be seated. Some people like it so much that they bring their lunch and make a day of it. There is going to be a fund raising dinner in the basement of the L.C. and they're going to use the money to buy more seats. Quite honestly, it pains me that I can't go more often...I know I should, but it gets more difficult when you get older...especially in the winter. So, you come down and stay at our camp, and maybe we can go with you the first time to the L.C. and sit by you. I'll introduce you to all the nice folks around here, because, after all, this is a very, very friendly community."

196. THE 11TH COMMANDMENT

SIGN IN PARKING LOT OF
ASSEMBLY OF GOD CHURCH

THOU SHALT NOT PARK — *Violators Will be Baptized.*

197. DO I HAFTA GO?

Junior: *"Dad, did you go to Sunday school when you were a little boy?"*

Father (smugly): *"I sure did. Never missed a Sunday."*

Junior: *"See, Mom? I'll bet it won't do me any good either."*

198. A GREAT PREACHER

After his standing ovation, the speaker was approached by a well-dressed member of the audience, *"That was the most inspiring motivational speech I've ever heard. I'll bet this talent has made you rich."*

Speaker: *"Thank you for your compliment. I've done real well, but I'm not in this for the money!"*

Man: *"You ought to be...you'd make a million dollars as a preacher!"*

Speaker: *"Yeah, but what would I spend it on?"*

199. BRIDLE THY TONGUE AND SADDLE MY HORSE

The old-fashioned preacher had built the congregation up to a heated fervor, "Confess, Repent," he shouted, "Tell all!"

From the back of the church rose a middle aged guy who had been moved to tears by the passionate appeal.

"Oh, Preacher," he shouted, "I am a terrible sinner, and I've done so many things to be ashamed of." He fell on his knees in the aisle.

"Tell it all," shouted the preacher and the congregation. "Tell it all!"

"I spent my last paycheck gambling, every last cent, playing cards," he confessed as he crawled halfway to the alter.

"Tell it all," shouted the church, "Tell it all!"

"I'm a drunkard," he cried as he crawled, "I spent all my family's rent money on sour mash whiskey and moonshine."

"Tell it all," they cried, "Tell it all!"

Bracing himself at the alter, perspiration dripping from him, shaking with emotion, his voice quivered, "Last night, I kissed a goat!!"

Silence quickly filled the church. The preacher looked down and said, "Brother, I don't believe I'd a told that!"

200. HE'S AT MY PLACE

"Where does God live?" asked the Sunday School teacher of a little four-year-old boy in her class.

"In our bathroom," replied the youngster very matter of factly.

"In your bathroom," asked the amused teacher. "Why do you say that?"

"'Cause, every morning my dad goes to the door and yells, 'Good Lord, are you still in there?'"

201. GET THE MESSAGE

An especially pious preacher parson called on a couple of boys who were widely-known in the community as being troublemakers.

The parson asked, "Do you two fellows have any idea what good clean fun is?"

"I'll bite," answered one. "Tell us, what good is it?"

202. GOD ONLY KNOWS

Two deacons were having a social drink at a bar when they saw their preacher pass by the window. One of them became very upset.

"Oh, surely he didn't see us!" he worried.

"What difference does it make?" his friend replied. "God knows we're in here."

"I know," said the first deacon, "but God won't tell my wife!"

203. I KNOW, I KNOW

The little girl in Sunday School was paying close attention to the teacher's lecture on the power of prayer.

"And what must we do before God forgives us?" asked the teacher.

"Sin," said the little girl brightly.

204. HAPPY TO GO

A woman was giving her testimony: "Before I joined the church, I just hated my brother-in-law. I hated him so much I wouldn't have even gone to his funeral, but now that I'm a church member, I am ready to go any day."

205. SIGN ME UP

Notice on a church bulletin board: "Work for the Lord. The pay is not much but the retirement plan is out of this world.

206. BE KIND

At the local restaurant after church, two arm chair deacons were reviewing the sermon. First member: I thought the sermon today was unique. It reminded me of the peace of God. It "passed all understanding".

Second member: It reminded me of the mercies of God. I thought it would endure forever.

207. GO, GO

Some bring happiness wherever they go, others whenever they go.

208. LOOKY THERE

If you want to know what God thinks of money, look at the people he gives it to.

209. TACTFULLY

The ladies group members were discussing their new minister. Ethel reported that the handsome young reverend had paid her a compliment..."He said I looked like a breath of Spring."

Mabel snorted and said, "Ethel...that's not exactly the way he put it. What he SAID was...you looked like the end of a long, hard winter."

210. COMMUNICATION

In a Moscow park, an elderly Jewish man was studying Hebrew. A Russian soldier, passing by, remarked, "What are you studying Hebrew for? When you die, you won't go to Israel."

The man replied, "So, I can use it in heaven."

The Russian soldier asked, "What if you end up in hell?"

The old man said, "Big deal. I already speak Russian."

The Time Of Your Life:

Strange People
I Have Known

211. GOT A DRAWL, YA'LL?

An Aggie who had a very heavy Texas drawl was trying to learn to talk like other Americans where he was living in Iowa. Seems that everywhere he went, people spotted him as a Texan because of his accent. So, the Aggie spent $750 on diction lessons, hoping to sound like an average American.

After his final lesson, the Texan decided to try out his new diction by going shopping. He went into a store and approached a clerk.

"I would like to buy...a pound of butter...a dozen eggs...three pounds of ground round...and a ring of Wisconsin cheese," said the Texan, in perfect Midwestern style.

"You're an Aggie, aren't you?" asked the clerk.

"Yes, I am," he answered in perfect diction. "But, how could you tell?"

"'Cause you're in a Feed store!" yelled the clerk.

212. HUNTING WE WILL GO

A Texas Aggie friend of mine recently got killed while he was out hunting? He was following some tracks...and got hit by a train!

213. DRINKING LESS

It's true that Aggies drink less Kool-Aid than folks in all other states.

The reason is, they have such a hard time getting two quarts of water into that little bitty envelope.

214. MATH WHIZ

"How much are yer apples?" asked the Texas Aggie.

"All you can pick for one dollar," said the rancher.

"Okay," said the Aggie, "I'll take two dollars' worth."

215. WHAT A COOK!

An Aggie friend of mine told me that his wife's cooking is gettin' a lot better than it used to be. He knows that's true, 'cause he came home early from work yesterday and a truck driver was there eatin' lunch.

216. ON YOUR TOES

Hank is an eccentric old bachelor who doesn't get out much. Last week, I took him to the ballet. "What'd you think," I asked him after the standing ovation.

"Well, he said, "it looks to me like instead of having those poor girls dance on their toes, they ought to hire taller girls."

217. I SEE YOUR POINT

Judge: "I don't blame you for wanting to change your name from Joe Hogbristle. What name do you want to use?"

Joe: "Harry Hogbristle. I'm sick and tired of folks asking "Whataya know, Joe?"

218. NO DANGER

Wife: You know the old saying, "What you don't know won't hurt you"?

Husband: What about it?

Wife: You must really be safe.

219. STOP THAT

I found out how to keep a hillbilly girl from biting her nails.

Make her wear shoes!

220. TRUE JUSTICE

Judge: You've been brought here for drinking.

Jake: Swell!! Let's get started!

221. LOOK SMART

Intelligence is very much like money - if you don't let on how little you've got, people will treat you as though you had a lot.

222. THE THINKER

He always uses his head. He knows it's the little things that count.

223. DANGEROUS MIX

He combines the wisdom of youth with the energy of old age.

224. HALF COLD

My neighbor bought only one snow boot for winter. He heard there was going to be only one foot of snow!

225. KEEP IT

He left his brain to Harvard Medical School. They are contesting the will.

226. HIGH WIND

I'm not too confident in my new mechanic. Yesterday he changed the air filter in my car...he said he never could understand how the air got from there all the way down to the tires.

227. DUCK!

Overheard: "To damage his brains, you'd have to hit his wife in the head."

228. SWITCH

He just opens his mouth long enough to change feet.

229. COMMON SENSE

Beverly: A scientist says that what we eat we become.

Melba: Oh boy! Let's order something rich.

230. A GOOD DEAL

"I just bought a two-story house. The salesman told me one story before I bought it and another story after I bought it."

The Time Of Your Life:

My Health And Medical Experiences

231. GOOD NEWS, BAD NEWS

Doctor: I have some good news and some bad news. Which do you want first?

Patient: Give me the bad news first.

Doctor: We amputated the wrong leg.

Patient: What is the good news?

Doctor: Your other leg won't need to be amputated after all.

232. WHAT DAY IS THIS

People who think that time heals everything haven't tried sitting it out in a doctor's waiting room.

233. LAND OF THE FREE, HOME OF THE FED

We've got it pretty tough in America — half our income goes to buy food...the other half to lose weight.

234. LOOKS GREAT ON YOU

Two young men, Jack and Charlie, had gone through high school together. Both had good jobs. One morning, Jack called Charlie and said, "They've got me."

"Who's got you?"

"The army. But I am going to fool them at the physical. I once had a hernia, and I am going to wear my truss."

So Jack, wearing his truss, went down to the draft board. Three doctors examined him, and gave him a card that said "M.E." Jack said, "What's that?" They said, "Medically Exempt."

Four weeks later bright and early in the morning, Charlie called Jack and said, "They got me, too. You got out of it now how am I gonna get out of it?"

"Here, I'm not gonna use my truss anymore. You go down and make the usual complaints that you can't lift things, you have intermittent pains, and they will let you off for having a hernia."

Charlie went to the draft board. The same three doctors examined him and then handed him a card that read "M.E."

"Medically Exempt?" asked Charlie.

"No," replied the doctor. "Middle East. Anyone who can wear a truss UPSIDE DOWN can certainly ride a camel and 'pack a rifle'!"

235. MOTIVATIONAL DOCTOR

Jake had been going to the doctor and on the most recent occasion, the doctor advised him to eat less, work harder, and not go on any vacations.

"Will that help my condition?" asked Jake.

"Well, no," admitted the doctor, "but it will help you pay your bill sooner."

236. THE FINAL NOTES

He hadn't been feeling well, so he went to the doctor for a physical and came home with an electrocardiogram in the form of a long paper roll. His wife came home later, found the paper roll. Not knowing what it was, she put in on the player piano and it played "NEARER MY GOD TO THEE."

237. A GREAT PHYSICIAN

My Brother-in-Law, a Doctor in Texas, recently reported a great medical breakthrough. He performed the first successful hernia transplant...moved it from the right side to the left side.

238. DON'T WORRY

Doctor: Your leg is swollen, but I wouldn't worry about it.

Buck: If your leg was swollen, I wouldn't worry about it either.

239. YOU SAID IT

The expression most often heard in a Texas hospital operating room is "OOPS"!

240. TRYING TO HELP

Harry woke up after his operation and all the shades were down. "Why is it so dark?" the doctor replied, "There's a big fire across the street and I didn't want you to think the surgery had failed."

241. RIPE OLD AGE

After examining his new patient for the first time, the doctor said: "Mr. Jones, you are in fine shape. You should live to be 80."

"But I am 80," replied Mr. Jones.

"See?" said the doctor. "What did I tell you."

242. NO PAIN

Emerging from the dentist's office little Judy announced, "He's not a 'painless dentist' like you said he was."

"I'm sorry, " her mother answered, "Did he hurt you much?"

"Naw," the child shrugged, "but he sure yelled when I bit his thumb."

243. HOSPITAL SECRECY

Mr. Jackson had been in the hospital a long time. One night the phone rang at the night nurse's table. She said, "Hello," and the voice said, "Could you tell me how Mr. Jackson is doing?"

The nurse says "He's doing very well; as a matter of fact, he's being discharged tomorrow." And the caller said, "Thank you,"

The nurse said, "Who shall I say called?"

The voice said, "This is Mr. Jackson—the doctors don't tell me a cotton-pickin' thing!"

244. YOUR TURN

My brother-in-law is a doctor in New Mexico. He's different from most of 'em. He doesn't believe in all this unnecessary surgery. He never operates unless he really needs the money.

245. ALL IN MY HEAD

Patient: "Doctor, I think everyone tries to take advantage of me."

Psychiatrist: "That's silly. It's perfectly normal to feel that way occasionally."

Patient: "Is it really? Thanks for your help, doctor. How much do I owe you?"

Psychiatrist: "How much do you have?"

246. CORRECT DIAGNOSIS

The suffering patient looked at his doctor and asked: "Are you certain I'll pull through? I heard of a man who was treated for pneumonia and died of diphtheria."

"Don't be silly," said the doctor. "When I treat you for pneumonia, you die of pneumonia."

247. THE CURE

I was waiting to take my brother-in-law the doctor to lunch. A woman raced out of his office, red faced, walking fast, part of her underclothes under her arm, nearly knocked me down. "What did you tell her, Rex?" I asked my brother-in-law. "Told her she was pregnant," he replied. "Was she?" I asked. "Nope," he replied, "but it sure did cure her hiccups."

248. SHORT CHECK-UP

My Grandad only visited his dentist twice a year, once for each tooth.

249. WELL DONE!

Doctor Mann: "Congratulations, Dr. Williams, you performed the operation just in the nick of time?"

Doctor Williams: "Yes, in another twenty-four hours he would have recovered."

250. HYPOCRITIC OATH

I've got the best doctor in the world—if he can't cure you he will touch up the X-rays!

251. CAN I COME BACK AGAIN?

Nathan, my doctor brother-in-law in New Mexico, insisting on seeing a woman patient with a nurse, or with her husband, called in a couple at the end of his workday. He had a busy 10 hours of it. The woman spoke only Spanish, so he called in a nurse who interpreted that she had a mole on her stomach that was worrying her. The nurse left and, as was customary, the doctor had her remove part of her clothing, while the man stood. "That's just a little mole you've had all your life," he told her. The woman, who was strikingly attractive, threw on her clothes and rushed from the office. "Why is your wife upset?" asked the doctor of the man. "Wife? Never say her before in my life," he said. "I just came in for a flu shot."

252. THE BOTTOM

Whenever I go to see a doctor it's hard to forget that 50% of all practicing physicians today graduated in the lower half of their class.

253. CAME BACK

A doctor called my mother to tell her that her last check never cleared. My mother replied, "Neither did my arthritis."

254. SAGE ADVICE

It's okay to drink like a fish if you drink what the fish drinks.

255. HARD HEARING

My grandpa has trouble with his hearing. The doctor told him it's from drinking, and he had better give it up. But, as grandpa says, "I like what I drink better than what I hear."

256. IN A PICKLE

A group of prohibitionists looking for evidence of the advantages of total abstinence were told of an old man of 102 who had never touched a drop of liquor. They rushed to his home to get a statement. After propping him up in bed and guiding his feeble hand along the dotted line, they heard a violent disturbance from the next room — furniture being broken, dishes being smashed, and the shuffling of feet. "Good heavens, what's that," asked the visitors. "Oh," whispered the old man as he sank exhaustedly into his pillow, "That's Pa, drunk again."

257. NO TROUBLE

Psychiatrist: Are you troubled by improper thoughts?

Patient: No, I get a kick out of them.

258. IT WORKS

I'm on a new diet that is very effective. You only eat when there's good news.

259. PUMP THAT IRON

With Arnold Schwartzenegger chairing the President's Council on Physical Fitness, everyone is into fitness these days. A friend took up weight-lifting, got the broad shoulders, huge arms, muscular legs, rippling chest...she looks awful.

260. FEELING SO-SO

This is the age of the pill—pills to perk you up, pills to calm you down. I asked a friend the other day how he felt. He said he didn't know because he forgot which pill he had taken.

The Time Of Your Life:

Pets & Animals
I Have Owned
And Known

261. BEST FRIEND

The Aggie came home one day and shot his dog. When his neighbor expressed surprise, the Aggie explained, "Somebody wrote me a letter and said my wife was messing around with my best friend."

262. COLD WEATHER

During a bad cold spell last winter, my elderly neighbor let her two rabbits outside and they frozen to death. She took them down to the local taxidermist, set them up on the counter and said, "Could you do something with these?"

"I think so," he said. "Would you like them mounted?"

"No," she said. "I think holding hands would be fine."

263. CREATIVE ADVERTISING

Sign near zoo: For Sale-Elephant Fertilizer—for people who like trees with big trunks!

264. WHAT A DOG

An eccentric fellow smugly showed his neighbor an animal that appeared to be a dog. "He's unique!" he exclaimed. "He's part dog and part bull, and he cost a thousand dollars."

"Which part is bull?" asked the astonished neighbor.

"That part about the thousand dollars."

265. I'M NOT LION!

The hit of the circus was a beautiful female lion-tamer. She always had her animals under perfect control, and at her command the fiercest, wildest lion came meekly to her and took a lump of sugar from her mouth. The crowd thundered its applause, all except one man at the top, who had evidently had a few too many.

"Anybody can do that!" he yelled. The crowd got quiet.

"Would you like to try it?" shouted the ringmaster.

"Sure!" replied the man. "Get that lion out of there!"

266. LAZY

My neighbor says he has one rooster so lazy that when the other roosters crow, he just nods his head.

267. BREAK IT GENTLY

The driver, passing the cabin of a mountaineer, had the bad fortune to run over and kill a hound dog that happened to be the owner's favorite hunting dog. He went into the house and told the man's wife what had happened and how sorry he was. The owner of the dog was out in the field, and the motorist decided he had better go out and tell him of the accident, too.

"BETTER BREAK IT TO HIM EASY LIKE," advised the wife. "FIRST, TELL HIM IT WAS ONE OF THE KIDS."

268. RIDE OUT

The Eastern Democrat walked into a saloon in Texas and ordered four double whiskeys one right after the other. Thus fortified, he slowly got to his feet, looked down the length of the bar and yelled, "George Bush is a horse's behind!" Right away a big cowboy stalked down the floor. "Wait a minute," said the Easterner. "Why can't I say the President is a horse's behind? After all, this is a free country, isn't it?"

"You don't understand, mister," said the cowboy. "THIS IS HORSE COUNTRY."

269. YOUR RELATIVE

Trying to emphasize a lesson on charity and kindness during a fund raising dinner speech, the politician said, "If I saw a man beating a donkey and stopped him, what virtue would I be showing?"

"Brotherly love," shouted a voice from the back of the room.

The Time Of Your Life:

Divorces I Have Known About

270. MIGHTY NICE OF YOU

The Judge at the divorce proceedings turned to give his decision to the ex-husband, "Mr. Atwater, I'm going to award your wife 2,000 dollars a month."

Mr. Atwater, "That's mighty kind of you, your Honor; I'll try to chip in a little myself!"

271. GETTING ALONG

A friend of mine told me that his was a "friendly" divorce. He got to keep whatever fell off the truck when she drove away!

272. SHHHOOT!

Attorney during divorce proceedings: "Now tell the jury the truth please. Why did you shoot your husband with a bow and arrow?"

Wife: "I didn't want to wake the children."

273. CLOSE SEPARATION

In Ohio, a husband weary of his wife's persistent nagging, moved out of the house and into the barn.

There, for months, he enjoyed a bachelor-like existence. He continued to attend to the yard and other chores but he never went into "her house" and she never came to check up on "his barn."

But they spoke to each other, continued on good terms and once in a while she cooked dinner for him and put it at his door.

Friends seemed to understand the situation. Some told him he had done a pretty smart thing. "But why?" asked one, "Why don't you run off? You'd do well to be rid her."

"I dunno," the husband replied. "As a wife she's nothing. As a neighbor, she ain't half bad."

274. ALL VOW, NO WOW

"My husband has no outstanding vices," she said to the counselor, "but I'm going to divorce him."

"Remember," the counselor advised, "when you married this man, it was for life."

"I know, I know," she replied, "BUT FOR THE PAST FIVE YEARS HE HASN'T SHOWN ANY SIGNS OF LIFE."

The Time Of Your Life:

My Most Embarrassing Moment

275. THINGS ARE LOOKIN' UP

My friend Lowell is only 5'3" tall but it doesn't bother him. "I like to go out with tall girls," he says, "cause they keep me on my toes."

276. I'M LATE

The most lonesome feeling I ever had was when I had a wreck in college going the wrong way on a one-way street. The investigating officer asked me where I was going. I told him wherever it was I must be late because everyone else was already coming back.

277. MOUNT UP

The big-game hunter took his wife on his latest safari. After several weeks they returned. The sportsman had bagged a few minor trophies, but the great prize was the head of a huge lion, killed by his wife.

"What did she hit it with?" asked a friend admiringly. "That .303 Magnum rifle you gave her?"

"No," answered her husband dryly. "With the Jeep we hired."

278. HARD TO SEE

I bought my wife a new car. Three weeks later I came home from work and there it was in the driveway, flat tire, broken headlight, and crumpled fender.

"How'd that happen?" I asked.

"Ran over a beer bottle," she said.

"A beer bottle, didn't you see it?"

"No, the old man had it under his coat."

279. LET'S PUT IT THIS WAY

Never admit that you are fat. Just say you come in the large economy size.

280. WHAT A SIGHT!

I walked into a clothing store at the beginning of summer and said to the clerk, "I'd like to see a bathing suit in my size." And the clerk said, "So would I, brother, so would I!"

281. IT HAD TO BE YOU

A fat man was trying to get to his seat at the circus.

"Pardon me," he said to a woman, "did I step on your foot?"

"Had to be you," she answered, after glancing at the ring. "All the elephants are still out there."

282. FLATTERY WON'T

A man and his wife went shopping for a man's suit and as the salesman measured the husband's waist, she remarked, "It's amazing when you realize a coconut palm that wide at the bottom would be a least 90 feet tall."

283. I WON'T LOOK

Joe is always concerned about other people's safety. Walking through the woods one day he accidently stumbled on a bunch of girls skinny dipping in a farm pond. He said, "Pardon me, I'm not here to look at you...I just came to feed the piranha fish."

284. MILITARY COMMUNICATIONS

An Air Force major was promoted to colonel and received a brand-new office. The first day behind his desk, an airman knocked on the door and asked to speak with him. The colonel, feeling the urge to impress the young man, picked up his phone and said, "Yes, general, thank you, yes. I will pass that along to the President this afternoon. Good-bye, sir."

Then he turned to the airman and barked, "And what do you want?"

"Nothing, sir," the other replied, "I just came to hook up your phone."

285. MY TALK HAS SOME GOOD POINTS

A young lady, with a touch of hay fever, took two handkerchiefs with her to a dinner party, one of which she stuck in her bosom. At dinner she began rummaging to right and left in her bosom for the fresh handkerchief. Engrossed in her search, she suddenly realized that conversation had ceased and people were watching her, fascinated.

In confusion, she murmured, "I know I had two when I came."

286. GLAD THEY'RE GONE

The story is told of a drill sergeant who barked a command: "All right, you dummies, fall out!"

With much confusion and clatter, every man in the company except one fell out and scattered. The sergeant glared at the remaining recruit and said, "Well?"

The rookie smiled and replied, "There sure were a lot of them, weren't there, Sarge?"

287. WRONG QUESTION

What happened to that dopey blonde your husband used to run around with?

I dyed my hair!

288. GOOD REASON

According to the Family Bible, his ancestors went west by covered wagon. I've seen some of the old family pictures, and I fully understand why the wagon was covered.

289. QUICK SNAP SHOT

"Did you tell the photographer you didn't want your picture taken?"

"Yes, I did."

"Was he offended?"

"No, he said he couldn't blame me."

290. HUMILITY

Young girl to date: "Aren't you getting embarrassed? That's the fifth time you've gone for more food."

Young man: "Why should I be embarrassed? I just tell them I'm getting it for you!"

291. GOOD NIGHT!

Ken: I slept like a log.

Melba: Yes, I heard the sawmill.

The Time Of Your Life:

My Most Painful Experience

292. HUMILITY

The three most difficult things to do are to kiss your wife when she's leaning away from you; cross a fence when it's leaning toward you; and to be humble when someone gives you applause!

293. NOT YOUR FAULT

A friend of mine has only one arm and wears a hook. He went on vacation and stopped in a barbershop for a shave. The barber, in the course of his work, knicked and cut him six times as he questioned him about his visit. After he finished, the barber looked at him and asked: "Say, haven't I shaved you before?"

"Nope," said my friend, "I lost my arm in the war."

294. DANGEROUS

"My wife drives like lightning," said my friend.

"Fast?" I asked.

"No," he said, "she hits big trees."

295. BIG POLICY

Buck says that Ethel's mother is so fat that she needs GROUP insurance.

296. HOW MANY

I got on the scale and it said "Come back—when you're alone".

297. THE BIG HOPPER

I'm not saying he's fat, but he...looks like a kangaroo with all the kids home.

298. REAL COMPLIMENT

The wife had spent a long time preparing her husband a fancy meal. After eating, he sat in an easy chair and proceeded to read the evening paper.

Wife: "Typical! I spend hours in that kitchen cooking a fancy meal for you and what thanks do I get? Never a word of appreciation."

Hubby: "Well, the gravy was tender."

299. DUBIOUS HONOR

My brother-in-law was named Man of the Year, which should give you some idea about what kind of a year it's been.

300. THAT EXPLAINS IT

Wife: "I've got a stomach ache."

Husband: "That's because you haven't eaten. You're stomach is empty, so it hurts."

Wife: "Now I know why you have headaches all the time."

301. MEMORY LANE

The trouble with people who never forget is that they wind up married to people who never remember.

302. ASK AND YE SHALL

"My wife is always asking for money," complained a friend of ours. "Last week she wanted $200. The day before yesterday she asked me for $125. This morning she wanted $150.,"

"That's unbelievable," I said, "What does she do with it all?"

"I don't know," said our friend, "I never give her any."

303. THAT'S HOMELY

My cousin is really homely. One time she stayed overnight with us and when she went upstairs to bed, she forgot to pull down the shades. So the neighbors all pulled down theirs. When she rides in the car, the bugs won't even hit the windshield on her side.

304. SO LONG

At the first sign of trouble, he thinks with his legs.

305. PLAY WAS WORK

I never had friends when I was young. I hated to go to the park. I'll never forget the seesaw. I had to keep running from one end to the other.

306. I KNEW

How do you know your family was poor?

Every time I passed someone in town, they would say, "There goes Joe. His poor family!"

The Time Of Your Life:

My Travelling Experiences

307. SECOND CAR

"They don't build cars like they used too. We finally got the perfect second car — a tow truck."

308. TRAVELING HUSBAND

One of my business partners had been on the road travelling heavily for over 3 months. Finally, he decided to stay home with his wife for one straight week.

He told me she was so thrilled and excited on that first day, that every time the mailman or a delivery man came to the door, she shouted, "My husband's home, my husband's home!"

309. THE LUGGAGE IS LOST

You know you're in trouble when you go to the airline desk to complain about losing your luggage and the guy behind the counter is wearing your clothes.

310. FLY SLOW

Two women were preparing to board the airliner. One of them turned to the pilot and said, "Now, please don't travel faster than the speed of sound. We want to talk."

311. FLYIN' TIME

Pilot: Control tower, what time is it?

Control tower: What airline is this?

Pilot: What difference does that make?

Control tower: If you're United Airlines, it is 6:00 p.m.; if you're American, it is 1800 hours; if your Continental, the big hand is on the..."

312. HAULING HOGS

Did you hear that in Iowa they're establishing a railroad that will specialize in hauling only hogs? They're gonna call it Hamtrak.

313. DON'T KICK THE TIRES

What this country really needs is a car that gets 200 miles to the gallon and runs on junk mail and aluminum cans.

314. RIDE ON

Ruth rode on my Harley,
Directly back of me:
I hit a bump at fifty-five,
And rode on ruth-lessly.

315. DON'T CRITICIZE

"Honey, we must be getting close to town—you're hitting more people."

316. NEW MODEL

Two men were talking about the inventor of the first car.

"I think Henry Ford was the first man to invent a car," said one.

"No, he wasn't," the other replied. "The Bible says Moses came down from the mountain in his Triumph."

317. GOIN' IT ALONE

One of my friends always envied me for getting to go to great places around the country...especially Chicago. He always wanted to see Chicago.

Last week, I went by to see him to tell him I'd booked a speech in Chicago and see if he'd like to go along.

He was ecstatic, excited and enthusiastic! "We'll take my car!" he shouted. "Car?" I laughed, "We're not taking a car, I fly to these far away speeches."

His face dropped, "Then I'm not going," he said firmly, "'cause I don't fly." "You don't fly?" I asked in disbelief. "That's right. I don't fly and I don't swim...I don't do nothing that when you're doing it, if you stop, you die!"

318. HAND ME THE SOAP

The hotel clerk told the salesman that there were no more rooms with bath, and would he mind sharing a bath with another man.

"No," said the salesman, "not as long as he stays at his end of the tub."

319. GREAT MILEAGE

The other day I was driving under the influence of my wife. She talks and talks. She gets 10,000 words to the gallon.

320. ARE YOU THERE YET

Jim checked out of his hotel room and discovered that he had forgotten his umbrella. By the time he got back to his room, the hotel had rented the room to a young honeymoon couple. So before he knocked, he heard a wild conversation going on inside the room.

> *"Whose little hair is this?"*
> *"All yours, honey."*
> *"Whose little eyes are these?"*
> *"All yours, honey."*
> *"And whose little nose is this?"*
> *"All yours, honey."*
> *"And whose little mouth is this?"*
> *"All yours, honey."*

Jim, standing outside, couldn't contain himself any longer, and yelled through the door, "When you come to an umbrella, that's mine!"

321. NOW I SEE

On a recent trip to Washington, I finally learned what the initials 'D.C.' stand for: Darkness and Confusion.

322. TAKE YOUR PICK

Customer: I don't like all these flies that are buzzing around here.

Waiter: Well, just point out the ones you do like, sir, and I'll swat the rest.

323. CATCHY SIGN

Sign in a restaurant window: If you don't eat here, we'll both starve.

324. STEP FORWARD

Then there was the waiter who backed into the meat grinder and got a little behind in his orders.

325. READ THE SIGN

Some signs in those cafes that brag about having "home cooking" makes one wonder what sort of home the cook came from.

326. SECOND CHOICE

Tourist (looking over menu): "Hmmm...let's see...I'm having trouble keeping my weight down, so I think I'll try the chicken liver stew."

Waitress: "That makes two things you're gonna have trouble keeping down."

327. TAKE ME

"I know a place where women don't wear anything except a string of beads once in a while."

"Where?"

"Around the neck, silly!"

328. ME NO SAVVY

FOREIGNER (in drugstore): No, I want the small size.

CLERK: In America, sir, there are only three sizes: large, giant, and Texas size. If you want small, take the large.

329. THAT'S BIG

A guide was showing the sights of Chicago to a group of tourists. In the group was a Texan, who kept pointing out that he knew a place back home that was prettier, larger, had greener trees, or could turn out products cheaper and faster.

Finally they got to the Sears Tower Building. The guide announced, "Here stands the biggest building in the world. It's two miles to the top."

"That's nothin'," snorted the Texan "In mah hometown we got outhouses taller than that."

"I believe it," said the guide. "You need them."

330. OUTDONE IN THE OUTBACK

A Texan visiting Australia saw a kangaroo for the first time and drawled, "Ah'll grant you one thing for sure. Your grasshoppers are bigger than ours."

331. TEXAS AT LAST

An Englishman, thrilled at his first visit to Texas, stepped off the plane in Dallas and gazed around at the tall buildings. Stopping a passerby, he said, "I can scarcely believe I am in Texas. Is this really Dallas?"

The man smiled and nodded, "Si, senor."

332. JUST LIKE HER

Jack and I had been on the road for 2 weeks when we checked into a hotel in Amarillo. Jack saw a familiar figure across the lobby and said, "Dale, that lady looks just like my wife — Why I'll bet it is — she drove down here to surprise us!" He went over, grabbed her from behind and kissed her. As he did he realized his mistake. "I'm sorry," he said. "You look just like my wife." She shouted, "Get away from me you old coot!" "Gee," Jack said. "You talk just like her, too."

333. WELCOME TO NEW YORK

New Resident: "New York is such a friendly town. Last night we had three visitors—two while we were at home."

334. DOING OUR BEST

"Any big men born around here?" asked the tourist in a sarcastic way.

"Nope," replied the native. "Best we can do is babies."

335. NOT MUCH COMFORT

An astronaut preparing for a launch into space was asked how he felt. The astronaut replied, "How would you feel knowing you were going into space in an aircraft with over 140,000 parts and they were all supplied by the lowest bidders?"

The Time Of Your Life:

My Greatest Success

336. SUCCESS

You can always tell when an Okie starts doing well financially. He's got ash trays in his house with no advertising on them.

337. GOOD BYE

My wife is on a diet where she's losing five pounds per week. I've calculated in 30 weeks I'll be completely rid of her.

338. YOU WIN

I have been advised by a Russian friend in Moscow that they have just introduced a new million ruble lottery. The winner gets a ruble a year for a million years.

339. NO TIPPING

The young cowboy was raised in a proper home and his mother had taught him the art of courtesy. Occasionally he forgot his courtesy, but was able to draw on skills that got him out of trouble.

One day he happened to step on an elevator in Dallas in which he and a middle-aged fussy socialite were the only occupants. He forgot to take off his hat. When the snobbish woman asked, "Don't you take your hat off in the presence of ladies?," he quickly replied, "Only in the presence of old ones, ma'am."

340. AGAINST HER WILL

He didn't want to marry her for her money, but he didn't know any other way to get it.

341. NO DEBT NO CREDIT

Remember the good old days? A man was known for his deeds. Now he is known for his mortgages.

342. HOLLER FOR DOLLARS

If you want to be remembered, borrow money. If you want to be forgotten, lend it.

343. YOU'RE SO LUCKY

First Wife: "Gee, Myrtle, the bank returned my check."

Second Wife: "Are you ever lucky. What are you going to buy with it next time?"

344. PAPER COW

Trouble with most of us business owners today is that when we're rich it's usually on paper and when we're broke it's in cash.

345. GREATEST IN THE WORLD

The greatest salesman that I ever heard of was a milking machine salesman. He went out to see a farmer who had only one cow, sold him two milking machines and took the cow as a down payment.

346. REEL 'EM IN

A man in the insane asylum sat fishing over a flower bed. A visitor approached, and wishing to be affable, asked, "How many have you caught?" "You're the ninth," was the reply.

347. GOOD ADVICE

Smile—it adds to your face value.

348. MORE ADVICE

Keep smiling. It makes people wonder what you've been up to.

349. MILITARY HONORS

Reporter: And how did you win the Distinguished Service Cross?

Private: I saved the lives of my entire regiment.

Reporter: Wonderful! And how did you do that?

Private: I shot the cook.

350. SERIOUS STUFF

Whatever your years, there is in every being's heart the love of wonder, the undaunted challenge of events, and unfailing, childlike appetite for "what next," and the joy and game of life. You are as young as your faith, as old as your doubt; as young as your self-confidence, as old as your fear; as young as your hope, as old as your despair. In the central place of your heart, there is a recording chamber; so long as it receives messages of beauty, hope, cheer, and courage, so long you are young. General Douglas MacArthur

351. CUSTOMER SERVICE

Sign on a sanitation truck: "Satisfaction guaranteed—or double your garbage back."

352. ROLL ON

I tried a new deodorant called Invisible. The smell stays the same, but nobody knows where it's coming from.

353. NO RESPECT

"I get no respect from anyone. The other day the dog went to the door and started to bark. I went over and opened it. The dog didn't want to go out; he wanted me to leave."

354. NO BEEF

Word got out on the street that the local grocery store in Moscow was expecting a shipment of beef. By 9 o'clock in the morning, the line was 2 blocks long. By noon it stretch down the street and around the corner for 6 blocks.

At 2 p.m. the shipment had not arrived. The store manager said "We must reduce that line — go out and tell all the Jews they must go home — no beef for them.

By 4 p.m. still no beef. "Go tell the people any one who did not fight in any wars will have no beef and should go home." The line grew shorter.

By 6 p.m. still no beef. "Go tell the people any one who didn't fight in World War II, go home, no beef for you." The line grew even shorter.

By 8 p.m. still no beef. "Go tell the people any one who didn't fight in the Bolshevik Revolution, go home."

At 10 p.m. there are only 3 old men in line, practically frozen in the cold, snow falling on their heads and shoulders and chests full of medals. The store manager comes out and said, "We just got word, there will be no beef today. Go Home!"

One old soldier turned to his two comrades and says, "Those dadgum Jews, they get all the breaks!"

355. DAY JOB

A motorist, after being bogged down in a muddy road, paid a passing farmer $5 to pull him out with his tractor. When he was back on dry ground the motorist said to the farmer, "At that price I'd think you would be pulling people out of the mud day and night."

"Can't at night," replied the farmer. "At night I gotta haul water for the hole."

The Time Of Your Life:

My Worst
Failure

356. NO RESPECT

With my luck, if I had been a dog on Noah's Ark, I'd have ended up with both fleas.

357. IT'S WORKING

I've got a new exercise and a new diet. I go horseback riding every morning. It's working. So far the horse has lost 30 pounds!

358. DIFFERENCE OF OPINION

It's not that some folks aren't fat, their weight just settled in their hips.

359. I WANT MY MOTHER

The 70-year old man who was just about to celebrate his forty-fifth wedding anniversary decided to do it big with his wife. "Let's go back," he said, "to the Plaza Hotel, where we spent our wedding night, and celebrate. We'll order the same vintage French champagne and relive the whole thing." She replied, "That's wonderful, dear. And, you know, I still remember the number of the suite - 705." So they went back for their forty-fifth - same hotel, same champagne, same room, even the same kind of flowers in the room, roses. Only this time, HE went into the bathroom and cried.

360. DOW JONES DUMPS

My cousin, Elmer, made a killing in the market recently...he shot his broker.

361. NO FOOLIN'

About the old proverb "a fool and his money are soon parted.": I've always wondered how a fool and his money ever got together in the first place.

In fact, in Oklahoma, if you find a fool with NO money...he's probably running for office!

362. BIG IN OIL!

Nowadays when an Oklahoman says he "dabbles in oil", it means he works at a gas station!

363. WE MISS YOU

If you think nobody cares if you are alive...just miss a couple of car payments.

364. WRITE-OFF

The country is over a trillion dollars in debt, we spend more than we take in, and Congress has just given themselves a raise. Next year, I'm going to deduct last year's taxes as a bad investment!

365. CAN'T ALWAYS BE FIRST

Back in 1910 Governor Al Smith of New York was attending a Democratic conference in New York City. A succession of speakers went over the substantive problems of the day, and finally Al, who was the last speaker, found it was his turn. Al said, "I find that everything I was going to say has been pretty well covered. That's the handicap of being the last speaker-but after all you can't be the first in everything. Even George Washington, who was first in war and first in peace, married a widow."

366. BLAME THE BRITISH

Pity poor George Washington. He couldn't blame his troubles on the previous administration.

367. LOST HIS NOSE

The sportsman went to a hunting lodge and bagged a record number of birds with the help of a dog named "Salesman."

The following year, the man wrote the lodge again for reservations, requesting the same dog, "Salesman."

As soon as he arrived at the lodge, he asked the handler if "Salesman" was to hunt.

"Hound ain't no good now," the handler said.

"What happened?" said the man. "Was he injured?"

"Nope! Some fool came down here and called him 'Sales Manager' all week. Now all he does is sit on his tail and bark."

368. CALL FEDERAL EXPRESS

Old postmen never die, they just lose their zip.

369. BAD TIMING

"Why are you so downhearted?"
"I'm having some tough luck."
"How's that?"
"I got a check here for $40 that I'm trying to cash, and the only man who can identify me is a guy I owe $25 to."

370. HAT'S OFF TO YOU

"Why were you late back to camp, Private Anderson?" asked the Infantry leader.

"I'm sorry, Sarge," replied the Private. "But as we crossed that field of cows my beret blew off and I had to try on forty before I found it."

The Time Of Your Life:

Places I've Lived

371. IT'S TOUGH HERE

How bad's the drought? It's so dry here...
> *...the fish have ticks.*
> *...we have 2 year old fish that don't know how to swim.*
> *...the trees all lean towards the dogs.*

In fact, it's so dry here...
> *...the Baptists have started sprinkling,*
> *...the Methodists are using a wet washcloth,*
> *...and the Episcopalians are just spittin' on one another.*

372. WORDS OF WISDOM

Always put your hat on when you go to answer a knock at the door. If it's someone you want to see, you've just come in...if it's someone you don't want to see, you're just going out.

373. COME BACK AGAIN...SOMEDAY

Departing Guest: You've got a pretty place here, Frank, but it looks kind of bare.

Host: That's because the trees are rather young. I hope they'll have grown to a good size before you come again.

374. CHANGED HIS MIND

I'll tell you what our house is like. We have a priest living with us who wanted to get married. The Church sent him over to change his mind.

375. TAKE HIM HOME

My neighbor hasn't been out of our little town more than 30 miles in his life. I took him to Tulsa last week. He closed his eyes and ran out of the Sears Store when he saw a sign that read, "Women's Underwear - Half Off", and he thought Taco Bell was a Mexican telephone company.

376. HOME SWEET HOME

A small town is a place where everyone knows whose check is good and whose husband isn't.

The Time Of Your Life:

Death

(Other Than Speaking)

377. HE SURE LOOKS NATURAL

Two Texas Aggies attended the funeral of their friend Jake.

"He sure looks good," said one.

"He should," remarked the other, "he just got out of the hospital."

378. HONEST MISTAKE

"You say you want the death certificate changed, Doctor?" asked the puzzled clerk. "It's quite against the rules, you know."

"I know," replied the doctor, "but it's important. You see, I was in a hurry and didn't pay any attention to the space marked 'Cause of Death' and that's where I signed my name."

379. WHAT A FRIEND

One of my best friends is an undertaker...he's the last person in the world to let you down.

380. LAST RESPECTS

Cecil was playing his usual eighteen holes one Saturday afternoon. Teeing off from the 16th hole, he sliced into the rough over near the edge of the fairway. Just as he was about to chip out, he noticed a long funeral procession going past on a nearby street. Reverently, Cecil removed his hat and stood at attention until the procession had passed. Then he continued his game, finishing with a birdie on the eighteenth. Later, at the clubhouse, a fellow golfer greeted Cecil. "Say, that was a nice gesture you made today, Cecil."

"What do you mean?" asked Cecil.

"I mean it was really nice of you to take off your cap and stand respectfully when that funeral went by," the friend replied.

"Oh yes," said Cecil. "We would have been married thirty years next month."

381. JUST ONE

When Elmer retired, he and his wife Ruby moved to Phoenix. Once they'd settled in, he decided it was about time to make a will, so he made an appointment. "It's nice and straightforward," he instructed the lawyer. "Everything goes to Ruby—the house, the car, the pension, the life insurance—on condition that she remarries within the year."

"Fine, Mr. Adams," said the lawyer. "But do you mind my asking why the condition?"

"Simple," said Elmer, "I want at least one person to be sorry I died."

382. IT'S NOW OR FOREVER

Just after the civil war, a Southern gentleman found his wife in the arms of another man and, mad with rage, killed her with his revolver. A jury of his Southern peers had brought in a verdict of justifiable homicide, and he was about to leave the courtroom a free man when the judge stopped him.

"Just a point of personal curiosity, suh, if you're willing to clear it up."

In reply the gentleman bowed.

"Why did you shoot your wife instead of her lover?"

"Suh," he replied," I DECIDED IT WAS BETTER TO SHOOT A WOMAN ONCE, THAN A DIFFERENT MAN EVERY WEEK."

383. HEADSTONE HINDSIGHT

Beneath this stone lies Johnson.
They buried him today.
He lived the Life of Riley,
While Riley was away.

384. ETERNITY

A guy goes to his doctor to find out how his physical examination turned out.

And the doctor says, "I've got some bad news for you. You've got six months to live"

And the guy says, "Oh, my gosh, what am I going to do?"

And the doctor says, "If I were you I'd get married to a divorcee with small kids, move to South Dakota, and buy a farm."

And the guy says, "If I do that, will I live longer than six months?"

And the doctor says, "No, but it'll sure seem like it!"

385. GET IN LINE

But how about the Arab oil sheik with fifty wives who died waiting to get into a bathroom.

386. WHERE THERE'S SMOKE

"These are grandma's ashes."

"Oh, did the poor old lady pass away?"

"No. Just too lazy to get an ashtray."

387. POOR ME

At the funeral of one of the richest men in Texas, an obviously poor man wept the longest and loudest. A sympathetic bystander asked: "Were you a close relative?"

"No," sobbed the man. "That's why I'm crying."

388. GO HOME

St. Peter: "Where are you from, son?"

Man: "I'm from Texas."

St. Peter: "Well, come on in, but you ain't gonna like it."

389. IT'S MINE

"Hey!" cried Satan to the new arrival. "You act as if you owned the place!"

"I do," came the reply. "My wife gave it to me before I died!"

390. SHE'S A GEM

A little old lady who had lost her husband a few months ago was complaining to her Sunday School classmates about him not leaving her enough to live on. One of them saw a new big diamond ring on her finger and said, "Well, if he didn't leave you anything, where did you get that big diamond?" The little lady replied, "Well, in his will he left $5,000 for the casket and funeral, and $10,000 for the stone. That's the stone!"

391. SELF-INFLICTED

Ethel claims that Melba is a "suicide blonde"...dyed by her own hand."

392. A GREAT MAN

Farmer: "The greatest person who ever lived was Higginbottom,... brilliant, broad-minded, tolerant, generous, temperate; yet he died with his talents unsuspected."

Friend: "How did you manage to find out about him?"

Farmer: "I married his widow."

393. THE REAL REASON

"Hey, Ted, how you been doing?"

"Not too good. Had to bury my wife."

"Aw, I'm sorry to hear that. What was wrong with her?"

"Well, she was dead."

The Time Of Your Life:

Farmers And Ranchers

394. BREAKING THE NEWS

My brother-in-law has a great bedside manner with both patient and family. Last week he took a patient's wife aside in the hall and broke the news. "I'm afraid your husband will never be able to work on the farm again."

The Wife said, "Great! I'll go right in and tell him. It'll cheer him up."

395. FUNNY LOOKIN' COW

A group of inner city residents had taken a trip to the country with their kids to look at farm animals. "How come that cow doesn't have horns?" asked one lady to the farmer.

The farmer explained, "Well, some cows have horns and some don't. Some are born with horns and we dehorn them. Some breeds aren't supposed to have horns. There are lots of reasons why cows don't have horns, but the main reason why that cow don't have horns is 'cause it ain't a cow. It's a horse."

396. LAWYER VS. FARMER

The young attorney's first job was with a large railroad company. It wasn't long until he had his first case to try. A farmer noticed that his prize cow was missing from the field through which the railroad passed. He promptly went down and filed suit against the railroad company for the value of his cow.

In due course, the case came up for hearing before the local justice of the peace in the back room of the general store, and the smart young attorney came down from the big city to defend the railroad company. The first thing he did was to take the farmer, who had no attorney, over into a corner and begin talking to him about settling the case. Well, the young lawyer talked and talked and finally twisted the old farmer's arm so that the farmer, very reluctantly agreed to accept half of what he was claiming to settle the case.

After the farmer had signed the release and taken the check, the young lawyer just couldn't resist gloating over the old farmer a little bit, and he said, "You know, I hate to tell you this, but actually I put one over on you this morning. I couldn't have won that case. The engineer was asleep, and the fireman was in the caboose when the train went through your farm that morning. I didn't have one witness to put on the stand."

The old farmer smiled a bit and went on chewing his tobacco. Then he said, "Well I'll tell you young feller, I was a little worried about winning that case myself. You know that durned cow came home this morning."

397. KINDA DRY

Traveling through the Texas Panhandle, a salesman stopped for gas and got into a conversation with an old settler and his son. "Looks like we might have rain," he said.

"Hope so," said the old settler, filling the tank. "Not so much for me, but for my boy here. I've seen it rain."

398. TURN AROUND

It was so windy at home the other day, I saw a chicken, backed up against the wind, lay the same egg 5 times!

399. HIGH WIND

I don't mean to imply that it's windier where I live than where you live, but my neighbor never could get his tomatoes to ripen cause the sunlight kept blowing off of 'em.

400. ROUND UP TIME

The wind caused my cattle to get out yesterday. It didn't blow the barbed wire down, but it did blow all the barbs down to the corners.

401. COLD START

One winter morning, the farmer heard his wife trying unsuccessfully to start her car. He went outside and asked, "Did you try choking it?" "No," she replied, gritting her teeth, "but I sure felt like it."

402. INVOLUNTARY TERMINATION

I had to fire my foreman. He figured he ought to have high wages on his first job, because it's harder work when you don't know anything about it.

The real reason I fired him was because he got so bowlegged he couldn't keep his calves together.

403. PLOWED UNDER

We farmers need all the help we can get. As Pope John, whose own roots were in the soil, once said, "People go to ruin in three ways - women, gambling, and farming. My family chose the slowest one."

404. THANKS

As he rose to speak, the farmer got a rousing round of applause. "I appreciate your welcome. As the cow said to the farmer one winter morning. 'Thank you for the warm hand.'"

405. ALTERNATIVE AGRICULTURE

Times have gotten so tough in Oklahoma, that farmers are trying new enterprises. An Oklahoma farmer placed this ad in the Anchorage paper: "WANTED: 250 acres in Alaska to lease between November and March. Want to raise frozen vegetables."

406. NOT TO WORRY

You get out of life what you put into it.

I recall one time a friend of mine wanted to board his horse for a short while.

The first farmer he approached said he would keep it at $25 a day, plus the manure.

Too high, my friend thought, and went to another farmer, whose price was $15 a day, plus manure. Seeking yet a cheaper price, he went to a third, who offered to board the animal at $5 a day.

"How come you didn't ask for the manure, too?" my friend asked. The third farmer replied, "FOR FIVE DOLLARS A DAY THERE WON'T BE ANY."

407. THE CREAM OF THE CROP

Sign in front of a dairy farm: "Bought and Prayed For."

408. TOO MUCH PAPERWORK

It seems the government runs everything in farming. Official (in government office): "Now, sir, will you please fill in your name and address on this form?"

Farmer: "I knew it. I knew there'd be a lot of government red tape."

409. NEW CROP

"I'm going to diversify—I'm getting a job in town."

410. COME ON IN

A farmer stood at the Pearly Gates,
His face all ruddy and old;
"What have you done," Saint Peter said,
"To gain admittance to the fold?"

"I've been a farmer, sir,
I've farmed for many a year."
He slowly raised his hand to his cheek
And brushed away a tear.

The Pearly Gates swung open wide,
Saint Peter rang the bell;
"Come in, old man, you're welcome here,
You've already been through h ___ ."

411. RISE AND SHINE

Two neighboring farmers were continually digging at one another by bragging about how early they rose and started doing their chores.

Finally, to deal the final blow, Farmer Tuttle had his wife call Farmer Howe at 3 a.m.

"Is Mr. Howe there?" she asked, when Mrs. Howe answered the phone. "My husband just finished breakfast and would like to speak with him.

Silence on the other end. Then Mrs. Howe replied "Gee, I'm not sure where he is now, but he was around here this morning!"

412. MY FIRST ACT

The instructor at a first-aid course asked a dairyman, "What would you do if you found you had rabies?"

Answered the dairyman without hesitation: "Bite my inspector."

413. WASTED MONEY

Farmer: "You accuse me of spending too much on the farm? When did I ever make a useless purchase?"

Wife: "Why, there's that fire extinguisher you bought a year ago. We've never used it once."

414. TAKE ME TO THE CLEANERS

Nowadays when you hear of someone making a living from the soil, he's probably the owner of a laundromat.

415. HARD TO SAY

A farmer and his wife, married happily for almost half a century, were sitting in the front porch swing in the cool of the evening. The sun was going down in a blaze of color, the birds were trilling their evening song, the soft breeze wafted the scent of honeysuckle across the porch. The moment was a moving one. The farmer felt strangely moved to speech, and blurted out, "Coralee, sometimes I love you so much I can hardly keep from telling you."

416. BEWARE OF THE PIG

The Secretary of Agriculture was driving through the country on a narrow road when he met a lady driving on his side of the road. He swerved, she swerved, he swerved back and they passed each other on their proper sides.. As they passed she stuck our her head and screamed "pig" at the top of her voice.

Not to be out done he stuck out his head and yelled "sow". Then he topped the next hill and ran over a 275 pound pig!

He stopped, jumped out and apologized to the farmer standing nearby. "Don't worry," said the Secretary, "I'll replace your pig." "You can't," replied the farmer. "You're too dang ugly."

417. STAND THE HEAT

Three men who died were cremated. One from Nebraska, one from Iowa and one from Kansas. The Nebraska man was first. And when his ashes were removed, they were put into a quart jar. The Iowa man was next. His ashes were put into a pint jar. The Kansas man was last. At the end of 15 hours, the furnace door was opened. Out walked the Kansas man, mopping his face with his handkerchief and saying, "Boy, if we get two more days of this hot weather, it'll ruin the entire wheat crop."

418. MY WAY IS BETTER

"What are you doing with that manure?" said the city boy to the gardener. "I'm putting it on my strawberries," replied the gardener. "Really?" said the city boy. "Where I live we put cream on them!"

419. NO BULL

A city chap was crossing a pasture.

"Say there," he called to the farmer, "is this bull safe?"

"He's a lot safer than you are," was the reply.

The Time Of Your Life:

Lawyers

420. YOU'RE ALL CROOKS

A woman who was none too happy about being called for jury duty was being examined by the lawyers.

Asked if she knew the prosecutor, she growled, "Yep and he's a crook!"

Asked if she knew the defense lawyer, she snapped, "Yes, I know him and he's a crook, too."

At that point in the proceedings, the judge called both attorneys to the bench and whispered, "If either one of you asks her if she knows me I'll fine you both for contempt of court."

421. NO DEFENSE

Mr. Eberhardt, charged with embezzlement, arrived alone in court on the day of trial.

"Why is it that you are without benefit of counsel?" asked Judge Rodriguez.

"I did hire an attorney, Judge," explained Eberhardt, "but when he realized I didn't steal the thirty thousand bucks, he booted me out of his office."

422. DEFINITION OF LAWYER

Someone who helps you get what's coming to him.

423. GRANDAD'S OBSERVATION

One lawyer in a small town will starve to death...
...but two can make a dadgum good living...suing one another.

424. ONE-ON-ONE PRACTICE

A few months after setting up their own practices, the recent law school graduates got together to compare notes. "How's it going?" asked Mossman.

"Not bad," Mitchell confided. "I've got one client."

Mossman frowned. "Is he well off?"

"He was."

425. I KNOW 'EM

"Do you happen to be acquainted with any members of the jury?" asked the prosecuting attorney.

"Well, yes," replied the witness, looking over at the jury box. "With more than half of them, in fact."

"Keeping in mind the solemn oath you made before this court," pursued the attorney, "can you swear you know more than half of them?"

"I sure can—in fact, I'll swear that I know more than all of them put together."

426. 911 AND AWAY YOU GO

I have a lawyer friend who was so successful he had his own ambulance?

427. WE GOT ONE

A fellow got sick of city living and moved out to a small town. Some trouble followed him, though, so not much later he went into the general store and told the proprietor that he needed some legal advice. "Have you got a criminal lawyer here in town?" he asked.

"I reckon we do," admitted the storekeeper, scratching his grizzled chin. "But I don't know as we can prove it on him."

428. POUR POUR

What do you need when you have three lawyers up to their necks in concrete?

More concrete.

429. EENIE MEENIE MINEE MOE

Why does Washington, D.C. have the most lawyers per capita and New Jersey the most toxic waste dumps?

New Jersey had first choice.

430. SHOULD I?

An elderly, blind old woman retained the local lawyer to draft her last will and testament, for which he charged her two hundred dollars. As she rose to leave, she took the money out of her purse and handed it over, leaving a third hundred-dollar bill by mistake. Immediately the attorney was faced with a crushing ethics question:

Should he tell his partners?

431. NEW TRIAL

"Why is it that you want a new trial, Counsel?" asked the judge.

"On the basis of new evidence of a highly significant nature," replied the attorney.

"Oh? And what is the nature if this evidence?"

"My client has come up with twelve hundred dollars I didn't think he had."

432. PICTURESQUE

My attorney has a photographic mind. It's just never been developed.

433. HANGIN' IN THERE

At the barber shop, Dr. Smithton found himself in the chair next to the town banker, who inquired as to how his attorney was faring after suffering a heart attack.

"Not doing too well," the doctor replied solemnly. "In fact, Mr. Franklin is lying at death's door."

"Now isn't that too bad," commented the banker. "At death's door, and still lying."

434. A FIGHT TO THE FINISH

An attorney friend of mine in Nebraska named Bob Hallstrom had settled a very involved estate case and was telling me all the gory details. "It was a tough fight all the way," he boasted. "How's that?" I asked. "Well," he said, "The heirs got almost as much as I did."

The Time Of Your Life:

Old Age

435. NO FIRE IN THE FURNACE

Chico: Say, Charlie...your hair is getting kinda thin on top. Don't you think you maybe ought to get a toupee?

Charlie: Heck no. I don't see no sense in getting a new top for a convertible...when the motor's shot.

436. SAY AGAIN

My father-in-law says that being in his 60's isn't all that bad. In fact, he kind of likes being called a sexagenarian. At his age, it sounds like flattery.

437. STILL QUALIFIES

"Although he is retiring as chairman today, I think you will all agree that we won't let him leave our hearts. He has been much too important to us. It's like the time I overheard two young models talking about a wealthy bachelor. 'He's rich, I know,' said the first girl, 'but he's too old to be eligible.' 'No, he isn't,' her friend said. 'I think he's too eligible to be old.'"

438. HAPPY BIRTHDAY

My boss had a birthday last week. I tried to dig up some of his old friends for a party, and dig them up is about what I'd have to do.

He once got an award from the president...one of the few Calvin Coolidge gave out.

But we did have a great party! We tried to count the candles, but we were driven back by the heat.

439. OVER LOTS OF HILLS

I'm not saying my boss married late in life, but Medicare picked up 80% of his honeymoon.

He's at the age where his mind says GO, GO, GO, and the body says NO, NO, NO!

He reads Penthouse for the same reasons he reads National Geographic...to see places he'll never visit.

440. DOWN THRU THE AGES

There are three ages of man: youth, middle age, and "You're looking good".

441. PARTING SORROW

Know how to tell when you're getting old? When you go to bed at night there's more of you on the dresser than there is in the bed!

442. FEEL MY MUSCLE

A reporter interviewing a man who was believed to be the oldest resident in town.

"May I ask how old you are?"

"I just turned 100 this week," the oldster proudly replied.

"Great! Do you suppose you'll see another 100?" the reporter asked playfully.

"Well," said the man thoughtfully, "I'm stronger now than when I started the first 100!"

443. OLDER AND WISER

A man being interviewed by reporters on his 105th birthday was asked: "To what do you attribute your good health?"

"I don't know yet," he replied. "I'm still negotiatin' with two breakfast cereal companies."

444. BAD MEMORIES

Blonde to fellow worker: "I hate to think of life at forty."

Redhead: "Why? What happened then?"

445. HIGH PREMIUM

Fun is like insurance—the older you get the more it costs.

446. PREDICAMENT

Old Age: When your knees buckle but your belt won't.

447. ANY NEW BUSINESS?

"Come along with me, sonny, and I'll show you a good time at my birthday party today. If we light all the candles, they'll have to call out the fire department."

So the old fellow teetered out to the front porch and sat down in a rocking chair next to the spry-looking older woman.

"Hey, Sonny, how old are you?", she said.

"Sonny?", he said. "I'm no sonny. I'm 90 years old. How old are you?"

"My age is MY business."

"Well looks to me like, you've been in business a long time."

448. REAL OLD

You are an old-timer if you remember when a baby-sitter was called Mother.

449. SLY WIFE

My wife is really something. She never lies about her age. Instead, she just tells everyone she's younger than me; then she lies about MY age.

450. HAVE A DRINK

The weird scientist looked over reports on his life-preserving tonic.

"Hmmm," he mused, "I see where my elixir has had its first failure— a ninety-eight-year-old woman. Ahhh, but what's this! They saved the baby."

451. DIDN'T YOU FREEZE

Niece: Aunt Maudie, it sure got cold last night, I'll bet it made your teeth chatter.

Aunt Maudie: "Dearie, my teeth and I haven't slept together in years."

452. HI CUTIE

He's so old that when a girl flirts with him in a movie...she's probably after his popcorn.

453. SING

Aunt Mabel's favorite song, "Meet me under the clothesline, Darling, 'Cause that's where I hang out!"

454. NOTHING TO WEAR

My Grandad says the real reason women live longer is because they have whole closets full of dresses they wouldn't be caught dead in.

The Time Of Your Life:

Politicians

455. LOW PRESSURE FRONT

The politician was rushed to the hospital and an inexperienced nurse was assigned to him. She put a barometer in his mouth instead of a thermometer, and it read, "Dry and windy."

456. NEVER CLOSES

One of our former governor confesses he's getting a little concerned about the reputation he has as a talker. One restaurant owner, he said, put a candid picture of him with his mouth open in a window immediately below a sign reading: "Open 24 Hours a Day."

457. THE CHECK'S NOT IN THE MAIL

A filling station owner tried unsuccessfully for months to collect a bill from a politician. He finally sent a sob story to the debtor along with a picture of his little daughter. Under it he wrote, "This is why I need the money." By return mail the politician sent a picture of a beautiful girl in a bikini with the message, "This is why I can't pay."

458. PLEASE PASS

Actually, I do better at political dinners than some. At one function, my friend complained when he found out he was sitting between two State politicians. He said he makes it a rule never to sit next to a legislator. They never pass the right thing.

459. NAME SAKES

Senator Chauncey Depew was seated next to President William Howard Taft when the great after-dinner wit took note of Taft's obese girth. Looking at his awesome stomach, he said, "I hope if it's a girl Mr. Taft will name it for his charming wife."

To which Taft replied, "If it's a girl, I shall of course name it for my lovely helpmate of many years. And if it's a boy, I shall claim the father's prerogative and name it Junior. BUT IF, AS I SUSPECT, IT IS ONLY A BAG OF WIND, I SHALL NAME IT CHAUNCEY DEPEW."

460. BELIEVER

My Great-Grandad was a politician and lots of other things some of the family wasn't too proud of. He once observed, "It's useless to try to hold a person to anything he says while he is in love, drunk, or running for office."

461. I'M IN TROUBLE

A politician had finished a campaign speech when an enthusiastic woman yelled out, "You'll get the vote of every thinking American."

He said, "That's not enough—I need a majority."

462. VOTES FOR SALE

Politician: "My ethics will not permit me to accept your gift of a sports car."

Lobbyist: "Well, how about if I just sell it to you for, say, $25?"

Politician: "Great! In that case I'll take two."

463. VIVA LA PRESIDENT

I recently had the pleasure of sharing the platform with the President. I was pretty thrilled until I began to think about who was running the country while he was out of town.

A few months later I saw the Vice President in action at a press conference.

"Mr. Vice President, what do you think about Defense?", they asked.

"I'm a white picket man myself," he replied. "Next question."

"What do you think is the best naval destroyer?", was the follow-up question.

He thought a while and said, "A hula hoop with a nail in it."

464. WON'T TAKE LONG

The Secretary of Agriculture was on a country side tour when he asked a farmer for the loan of a quarter to call a friend. A weathered old hand thrust a hand deep into his worn out overalls and delivered this line: "Here's two. Call all your friends."